Jacob Brubacher

The Brubacher genealogy in America

Jacob Brubacher

The Brubacher genealogy in America

ISBN/EAN: 9783337220440

Printed in Europe, USA, Canada, Australia, Japan

Cover: Foto ©ninafisch / pixelio.de

More available books at **www.hansebooks.com**

THE
BRUBACHER GENEALOGY

IN

AMERICA.

BY

JACOB N. BRUBACHER,

ELKHART, Ind.
MENNONITE PUBLISHING CO.
1884.

PREFACE.

In the year 1868 a "Genealogy of the Brubacher family and connections" was written out for my own satisfaction, as also for future reference. In the year 1870, while visiting in Canada, Uncle John Brubacher (Deacon) earnestly requested that it should be printed, giving two dollars towards the expense. He succeeded in gaining the promise. To fulfill that promise, by the help of the Lord, the original has been rewritten and enlarged. Care was taken to gather reliable information. Any doubtful information was not accepted. Notwithstanding, errors will be found, because of incorrect information. Whenever a —— occurs the necessary information could not be ascertained. The figures enclosed, thus (1) indicate the generation in America, thus: (1) John Brubacher, (1) Theodore Eby, &c., indicates that they were the first generation in America. Hoping all honor will be given to the Lord, the "Genealogy" is now respectfully submitted to the public.   JACOB N. BRUBACHER.

Mount Joy, Lancaster Co., Pa., 1883.

THE
BRUBACHER GENEALOGY.

(1) JOHN BRUBACHER.
(FIRST GENERATION IN AMERICA.)

(1) JOHN BRUBACHER emigrated from Switzerland, Europe, to America about the year 1710. On the 27th of September, 1717, he, in company with Christian Hershey, took out a warrant of 1000 acres of land, lying on the Little Conestoga, in West Hempfield Twp., Lancaster Co., Pa. Here on this tract of land, John Brubacher built the first grist and saw mill in Lancaster Co.

In the year 1718 John Brubacher and Christian Hershey divided the above tract of 1000 acres into two equal shares of 500 acres each by a line east and west, Brubacher getting the southern half and Hershey the northern half. Whether John Brubacher was married when he came to America cannot be ascertained.

In the year 1729, May 13th, John Brubacher and his wife Anna, sold and conveyed 150 acres of the above 500 acres, on which were erected the grist and saw mill, to Christian Stoneman. Tradition says, he was under the impression that the " Milling business" has a tendency to lead men into dishonesty.

This John Brubacher and his wife Anna had nine sons and one daughter, as follows :
(2) John, (2) Jacob, (2) Abraham, (2) Peter, (2) Daniel, (2) Henry, (2) Joseph, (2) David, (2) Christian, (2) Anna.

(2) Anna Brubacher was married to Abraham Buckwalter.

(2) John and (2) Daniel settled on 300 acres of land at the Hammer Creek, in Warwick Twp., Lancaster Co., Pa., which their father had bought of Lewis and Mary Lewis, October 29th, 1731.

(2) Peter settled in Rapho township, Lancaster Co , Pa., near what is now Mastersonville.

(2) Abraham settled in Virginia, what is called Masonotta about 20 miles southwest of Winchester.

(2) Christian, (2) David, (2) Henry, (2) Jacob and (2) Joseph remained in the vicinity where their father lived, namely, West Hempfield township, Lancaster Co.

(2) Daniel Brubacher.

(SECOND GENERATION IN AMERICA.)

The following is a sketch of (2) Daniel Brubacher and his descendants :

(2) Daniel Brubacher married a daughter of Michael Doner. Their children are :

(3) John Brubacher, married to Elisabeth Bomberger. Their children are: (4) Christian Brubacher, married to Anna Horst. Their children are, (5) Abraham, (5) Fannie.

(4) Daniel Brubacher married Elisabeth Bucher. Their children are, (5) John, (5) Elisabeth, (5) Susan, (5) Fannie.

(4) Joseph Brubacher married Maria Bucher. Their children are, (5) Catharine, (5) Joseph, (5) Barbara, (5) Mary, (5) David, (5) Elizabeth, (5) Levi, (5) Jonas, (5) John, (5) Anna.

(4) Elias Brubacher (died single), (4) Maria Brubacher (died single), (4) John Brubacher married Elisabeth Musser. Their children are (5) Anna, (5) Christian, (5) Moses, (5) Martin, (5) Anna, (5) Magdalena, (5) Fannie, (5) Mary.

(3) Daniel Brubacher married Elisabeth Stauffer. They settled in Lebanon Co., Pa., at a large spring. Their children are : (4)

Anna Brubacher married John Heisey. Their children are, (5) Elisabeth, (5) Barbara, (5) John, (5) Daniel, (5) Peter, (5) Christian, (5) Henry, (5) Joseph, (5) Susan, (5) Veronica, (5) Catharine, (5) Anna, (5) Mary.

(4) Christian Brubacher married Elisabeth Eberly. Their children are, (5) Jacob, (5) Mary, (5) Veronica, (5) Joseph, (5) Isaac, (5) Lydia, (5) Anna, (5) Christian, (5) Susan, (5) Elizabeth, (5) Mary, (5) Samuel (5) Christian.

(4) Peter Brubacher married Anna Hershberger. Their children are, (5) Polly, (5) Sarah, (5) Joseph, (5) Daniel, (5) Peter, (5) Henry, (5) Elisabeth, (5) Magdalena.

(4) Daniel Brubacher married Anna Forrer daughter of Daniel and Barbara Forrer. Their children are, (5) Preacher David Brubacher (mentioned in the "Nissley" family).

(5) Maria Brubacher married Jessie Krall. Their children are, (6) George, (6) Anna, (6) Fannie, (6) Mary, (6) John, (6) Susan.

(5) Elisabeth Brubacher, single.

(5) Anna Brubacher married Isaac Baer. Their children are, (6) Maria, (6) Daniel, (6) Anna.

(5) Barbara Brubacher married Jacob Hershey. Their children are (6) Samuel, (6) Anna, (6) Emanuel, (6) Barbara, (6) (6) David, (6) Daniel.

(5) Frany Brubacher married Samuel King. Their children are, (6) Seright, (6) Mary, (6) David.

(5) Catharine Brubacher married John Spahr. Their children are, (6) George, (6) Daniel, (6) Maria, (6) John, (6) Isaac.

(5) Magdalena Brubacher married Pre. Thomas Strickler, and afterwards Peter Smith.

(5) Daniel Brubacher married Elisabeth Huber. Their children are, (6) Fannie, (6) John, (6) Anna, (6) Mattie, (6) Lizzie.

(4) John Brubacher (Bishop) married Anna Wenger. They lived near Mamheim, Lancaster Co., Pa. Their children are, (5) Mary, (5) Anna, (5) Elisabeth, (5) Rebecca.

(4) Jonas Brubacher married Veronica Brubacher. Their children are, (5) Susan, (5) Abraham, (5) Joseph, (5) Daniel, (5) Jonas, (5) Samuel, (5) Veronica, (5) Lydia, (5) Rebecca.

(4) Benjamin Brubacher married Catharine Snyder. Their children are, (5) Moses, (5) Samuel, (5) Michael, (5) John, (5) Jacob, (5) Elias, (5) Anna, (5) Catharine, (5) Elisabeth.

(4) Elias Brubacher died single.

(4) Samuel Brubacher married Mary Baer. Their children are, (5) (names could not be ascertained.)

(4) Susan Brubacher married Henry Brubacher. They lived in Franklin Co., Pa. Their children are, (5) Samuel, (5) Daniel, (5) Susan, (5) Franey, (5) Eliza, (5) Caroline, (5) John, (5) Henry, (5) Anna, (5) Ezra, (5) Abraham.

(4) Jacob Brubacher married Susan E. Brubacher. This family will be described in another place.

(4) Henry Brubacher died single.

(3) Anna Brubacher married Michael Graybill. This family will be described in another place.

(2) Daniel Brubacher, the father of the above family died. His widow married Peter Eby. Their children are (counted 3rd generation): (3) Joseph Eby, married Elisabeth Breckbill. Their children are, (4) Abraham Eby, married Susan Brubacher, (4) Peter Eby married Maria Eby; (4) John Eby married —— Hershey; (4) Jonas Eby married Mary Wolf; (4) Catharine Eby married Jacob Eberly.

(3) Peter Eby was a hermit. He died in Elisabeth township, Lancaster Co., Pa, December 9th, 1836, aged 70 years, 8 months and 29 days. He directed the balance of his estate to be invested in bread and distributed among the poor.

(3) Susan Eby married Abraham Long.

They lived in Lebanon Co., Pa. No information of their family could be obtained. This closes the sketch of (2) Daniel Brubacher and descendants.

(2) JOHN BRUBACHER.
(SECOND GENERATION IN AMERICA.)

The following is a description of (2) John Brubacher and his descendants:

John Brubacher was born in the year of our Lord 1719, in West Hempfield township, Lancaster Co., Pa. He died April 9th, 1804, aged 84 years and 7 months. After he had grown to manhood he wished to go to Germany to seek himself a wife. His father sent him to Virginia for money—his father had land in Virginia. But when he returned from Virginia the neighbors had dissuaded his father from letting him go to Germany. The father died. Then (2) John went to Germany where he was received with joy. He married Maria Newcomer in the year 1750, eight days before Whitsuntide. He with his wife Maria, returned to America. His cousin Abraham Brubacher accompanied them. Abraham was so well pleased with the new country that he wrote enticing letters to his brothers and sisters who also emigrated to America. More of their friends followed from time to time. One of the main causes was that they were subjected to many persecutions because of their faith and non-resistant doctrine. They had confidence in the proclamations of William Penn, feeling assured if once in Pennsylvania they could worship the God of their fathers according to the teachings of God's Word and the dictates of their consciences; which was unto them a full and a complete recompense for all their losses and privations in forsaking their native land.

Abraham Brubacher settled at the Middle Creek, in Clay township, Lancaster Co., Pa. In course of time he wanted to build a grist mill there. He met with difficulties on account of the "Water Right" which so offended him that he moved away. He moved into the vicinity called Indiantown, not far from where Ephrata now is. Here he settled. Hence his descendants are called the "Indiantown Brubachers." He begat children. The name of one was Abraham. He was a Preacher. The name of another one was Christian.

His descendants of the "Indiantown Brubachers are all scattered far.

After (2) John and Maria Brubach r returned to America, they settled at the Hammer Creek in Warwick township, Lancaster Co. But they were not permitted to live long together. After the short space of thirty weeks his wife died, on the 15th of December, 1750. Her remains were buried in the garden at the house. In the course of time the house was torn down and the garden changed into a meadow. Hence her grave was in the meadow. In the year 1880, her remains (not much could be found any more) were removed to the " Brubacher family grave yard" on the same farm and the grave marked with a marble grave stone bearing her name and date of death.

(2) John Brubacher married as his second wife Maria Tauner, eldest daughter of Michael Tauner, (since changed to Doner) April 30th, 1751. (Maria Tauner was born February 11th, 1729, and died June 21st, 1802, aged 73 years, 4 months and 10 days.) Her sister was married to her husband's brother, (2) Daniel Brubacher.

(2) John and Maria (Tauner) Brubacher begat sons and daughters, viz: (3) John Brubacher was born February 19th, 1752 "Old Style". (He died March 30th, 1783, aged 31 years, 1 month and 11 days.) He married Anna Eby. Their children are, (4)

John, (4) Maria, (4) Anna, (4) Christian. (4) John Brubacher the eldest son settled near Frederick, in Maryland. He died about 1818.

(3) Anna Brubacher was born August 28th, 1753, "New Style." (She died September 17th, 1830, aged 77 years and 20 days.) She married John Mayer. They had 2 children.

(3) Maria Brubacher was born July 6th, 1756. She died July 12th, 1827, aged 71 years and 6 days. She married John Baer, of Elizabeth township, Lancaster Co., Pa. He died in 1802, aged 51 years, 7 months and 26 days.

(3) John and Maria (Brubacher) Baer begat children. (4) John, (4) Anna, (4) Benjamin, (4) David, (4) Maria, (4) Magdalena, (4) Susan, (4) Samuel, (4) Gabriel. (4) Samuel Baer, the next youngest of the children, married a Miss Weaver, daughter of George and —— Weaver. Their children are, (5) Gabriel, (5) George W., (5) Anna, (5) Maria, (5) John, (5) Magdalena, (5) Samuel, (5) Isaac.

(3) Jacob Brubacher was born June 11th, 1758. He died of yellow fever, August 31st, 1793, aged 35 years, 2 months and 20 days. He married, in the year 1781, Susan Erb, daughter of Christian Erb. She was born

March 17th, 1762, and died January 22d, 1844, aged 81 years, 10 months and 5 days. Her brothers and sisters are, Joseph Erb, Daniel Erb, John Erb, Abraham Erb, Jacob Erb, Benjamin Erb, Elizabeth Erb, Magdalena Erb, Anna Erb, Barbara Erb, Christian Erb.

As already remarked (3) Jacob Brubacher died in 1793. His widow remained in widowhood nearly 51 years. In the year 1809 she traveled to Canada West to visit her daughter Maria, married to Benjamin Eby, her parents, *three* of her brothers and *four* sisters, who were all living in Canada West—then a wilderness.

The names of her brothers and sisters living in Canada are, Jacob, Abraham, John, Elisabeth, Barbara, Anna and Magdalena.

In the year 1816 she went the second time to Canada, accompanied by her youngest son John, who was single. She remained in Canada two years, keeping house for her son, John, until he married. She then returned home to spend the evening of her life continuing the necessary preparation to exchange this life with eternity.

On one of her journeys over the Alleghenies, she killed a large rattlesnake with her cane, proving that she was a very courageous woman.

The following is a sketch of the rest of (2) John Brubacher's children.

(3) Abraham Brubacher, born February 22nd, 1760. He lived about two years and died.

(3) Magdalena Brubacher, was born December 12th, 1761. She died June 2d, 1832, aged 70 years and 21 days. She married John Bruckart, of Hempfield township, Lancaster Co., Pa. They lived awhile in Virginia. He died there. His family were then brought to Lancaster Co., Pa.

(3) Elisabeth Brubacher, was born November 16th, 1764. She died January 17th, 1803, aged 38 years, 2 months and 1 day. She married Christian Martin. They lived about half a mile north of Mount Joy, Lancaster Co., Pa. They had 12 children, of which the following grew up and were married, viz: (4) Maria Martin married to Joseph Hoffman; (4) Anna Martin, married John Kuhns; (4) Elisabeth Martin, married John Metz; (4) Christian Martin died single; (3) Barbara Martin, married Christian Metz; (4) David Martin, married Mary Erb.

(3) Veronica Brubacher was born March 29th, 1766. She died March 6th, 1824, aged 58 years, 1 month and 5 days. She married John Bomberger. Of this family

no correct information could be ascertained. It is supposed by some that John and Veronica (Brubacher) Bomberger settled in Lebanon Co., Pa.

(3) Barbara Brubacher was born October 18th, 1768. She died September 1846, aged 77 years and 11 months. She married Abraham Martin. Their children are, (4) John Martin, (4) Anna Martin.

(3) There were yet two more sons; one lived only about a quarter of an hour, and of the other, named Christian, nothing could be traced up.

WE NOW RETURN TO (3) JACOB AND SUSAN (ERB) BRUBACHER.

They commenced "keeping house" on the old "Brubacher homestead" in Elisabeth (part of Warwick) township, Lancaster Co., Pa. They afterwards moved to Ephrata township, Lancaster Co., to what is now called "Keller's Mill," which they owned; also the land. Here he died. After his death his widow and family returned again to the old "Brubacher homestead" where the family grew up, thence "starting in the world" for themselves. They had seven children, viz:

(4) Jacob Brubacher was born January 27th, 1782. He died July 30th, 1854, aged

72 years, 6 months and 3 days. He married, in the year 1807, Maria Eby, youngest daughter of Christian and Catharine (Bricker,) Eby, of Elisabeth township, Lancaster Co.. Pa.

Maria Eby was born October 12th, 1787, and died April 16th, 1864, aged 76 years, 6 months and 4 days. Her father was a son of Christian and Elisabeth (Meyer) Eby. Christian Eby was a son of Theodore Eby who emigrated from the "Pfalz," in Germany, in the year 1717. Christian Eby, son of Theodore, died September 15th, 1756. His wife Elisabeth died December 12th, 1787.

(2) Christian and Elisabeth (Meyer) Eby begat children, viz:

(3) Christian Eby, born February 22d, 1734. He died September 14th, 1807, aged 73 years, 6 months and 22 days.

(3) John Eby was born September 28th, 1737.

(3) Barbara Eby was born December 14th, 1740. Married Jacob Hershey.

(3) Peter Eby was born November 11th, 1742.

(3) Anna Eby was born January 4th, 1745. Married Christian Stauffer.

(3) Andrew Eby was born January 11th, 1747.

(3) George Eby was born December 11th, 1748.

(3) Elisabeth Eby was born August 12th, 1751. Married Jacob Hershey.

(3) Samuel Eby was born December 20th, 1752.

(3) Michael Eby was born December 29th, 1755.

(3) Christian Eby, eldest son of the above family, married March 13th 1760, Catharine Bricker, daughter of Peter Bricker. She died March 16th, 1810, in her 67th year.

(3) Christian and Catharine (Bricker) Eby begat children, viz:

(4) Elisabeth Eby, born March 13th, 1762. She married Joseph Bucher. Their children are, (5) Anna Bucher, married to Abraham Hostetter. Their children are, (6) Abraham Hostetter, (6) David Hostetter.

(5) Jonas Bucher married Susan Wittwer: their children are, (6) Elisabeth Bucher, married to Jacob Greider, and Christian Eby. (6) Mary Bucher married Jacob Erb. (6) Fannie Bucher married Henry Zug. (6) Anna Bucher married Henry Reist. (6) Leah Bucher married Seth Eby. (6) Joseph Bucher married Anna Shenk, and Catharine Risser. (6) Catharine Bucher married

Christian Hernly. (6) Jonas W. Bucher (Deacon), married Susan Bollinger.

(5) Elisabeth Bucher married Daniel Brubacher. Their children are, (6) Susan Brubacher married to Samuel Gsell, (6) Elisabeth Brubacher married to Peter Reist, (6) John Brubacher married to Molly Bomberger, (6) Fannie Brubacher married Augustus Sturgis.

(5) Maria Bucher married Joseph Brubacher. Their children are, (6) Catharine Brubacher, married to John Bomberger, (6) Joseph Brubacher married to Susan Rudy, (6) Barbara Brubacher married to Christian B. Snyder, (6) Mary Brubacher married to Christian E. Bomberger, (6) David Brubacher (Deacon) married to Lizzie Hess, (6) Anna Brubacher married to Jacob Sherk, (6) Elisabeth Brubacher married to Levi Weaver, (6) Levi B. Brubacher married to Elisabeth Shaeffer, (6) Jonas Brubacher married to Leah Keller, (6) John Brubacher married to —— Weidler.

(5) Susan Bucher married to Henry Becker. Their children are, (6) John, (6) Elias, (6) Henry, (6) Levi, (6) Israel, (6) Nancy, (6) Catharine, (6) Sarah, (6) Eliza.

(5) Barbara Bucher married Christian Weis. Their children are, (6) Andrew-

Weis, (6) Henry Weis, (6) Samuel Weis, (6) Christian Weis, (6) Eliza Weis.

(5) Veronica Bucher married George Huber. Their children are, (6) John Huber, (6) Christian Huber, (6) Matilda Huber married to John N. Eby, mentioned in the "Eby" family.

(5) Catharine Bucher married to Samuel Lehman (Deacon). Their children are, (6) Henry Lehman, (6) Catharine Lehman married to Samuel Longenecker, (6) Sarah Lehman married to David Beck, (6) Maria Lehman, (6) Sem Lehman, (6) Fannie Lehman, married to Henry C. Gingrich, (6) Elisabeth, (6) Samuel, (6) Jonas and (6) Susan—the last four died young.

(4) Christian Eby was born October 16th, 1763. He died August 27th, 1824, aged 60 years, 10 months and 13 days. On December 2d, 1788, he married Veronica Hershey, daughter of Christian and Anna Hershey. She was born November 19th, 1766, and died February 4th, 1826, aged 59 years, 2 months and 15 days.

(4) Christian and Veronica (Hershey) Eby begat children, viz:

(5) Catharine Eby, born December 17th, 1789; died April 17th, 1866, aged 79 years, 2 months and 14 days

(5) Anna Eby, born January 6th, 1791.

She married Samuel Nissly, (described in the "Nissly" family.)

(5) Elisabeth Eby, born February 21st, 1793. She died November 19th, 1863, aged 70 years, 8 months and 28 days. She married David Gingrich, son of David and Anna Gingrich. David Gingrich was born March 18th, 1791, and died July 24th, 1858, aged 67 years, 4 months and 6 days.

(5) David and Elisabeth (Eby) Gingrich begat children, viz:

(6) Anna E. Gingrich.

(6) Samuel E. Gingrich married Rebecca Schlott. Their children are,

(7) John S. Gingrich married Adaline Rutt. Their children are, (8) Dora, (8) Elmer, (8) Ella.

(7) Anna S. Gingrich married Albert Matzall. Their children are, (8) Barbara, (8) Amos.

(7) Rebecca S. Gingrich married Eli Metzler. Their children are, (8) Dora.

(7) Mary S. Gingrich married Harry Hess, (7) Susan S. Gingrich, (7) Barbara S. Gingrich, (7) Samuel S. Gingrich, (7) Jacob S. Gingrich.

(6) Fannie E. Gingrich married to Isaac Frank. Their children are, (7) Lizzie G. Frank, married to Benjamin Weaver, (7) Christian G. Frank.

(6) Elias E. Gingrich died single.
(6) Christian E. Gingrich. (Described in the "Stauffer" family.)
(6) John E. Gingrich married Anna B. Eby. Their children are, (7) Fannie Gingrich married to John Baer. (7) Lizzie Gingrich, (7) Jonas Gingrich, (7) Emma Gingrich, (7) John Gingrich, (7) Simon Gingrich, (7) Charles Gingrich, (7) Clara Gingrich, (7) Stella Gingrich.

(6) Benjamin E. Gingrich married Susan Smith. Their children are, (7) Henry S. Gingrich, (7) Emanuel S. Gingrich.

(6) Levi E. Gingrich married Katie Christ. Their children are, (7) Abner C. Gingrich, (7) Harman C. Gingrich, (7) Katie C. Gingrich, (7) Daniel C. Gingrich.

(6) Jacob E. Gingrich married Eve Smith. Their children are, (7) Ezra S. Gingrich, (7) Sallie S. Gingrich, (7) Willie S. Gingrich, (7) John S. Gingrich.

WE NOW RETURN AGAIN TO THE "EBY" FAMILY.

(5) Maria Eby was born February 1st, 1795. She died August 15th, 1880, aged 85 years, 6 months and 14 days. She married Peter Eby, son of Joseph and Elisabeth (Brechbill) Eby. Peter Eby was born in

the year 1799, and died in 1859, aged 60 years, 11 months and 29 days.

(5) Peter and Maria (Eby) Eby begat children, viz:

(6) Seth Eby, born January 30th, 1820, married November 2d, 1841, Leah Bucher, daughter of Jonas and Susan (Eby) Bucher, died October 31st, 1883, aged 63 years, 9 months and 1 day. Leah Bucher was born June 27th, 1816. Died December 12th, 1848, aged 32 years, 6 months and 27 days.

(6) Seth and Leah (Bucher) Eby begat children, viz:

(7) Susan B Eby married Abraham Lane. Their children are, (8) Jacob E. Lane, (8) Anna E. Lane, (8) Christian E. Lane.

(7) Mary B. Eby married Peter Ebersole. Their children are, (8) Seth E. Ebersole, (8) Anna E. Ebersole, (8) Susan E. Ebersole, (8) Peter E. Ebersole.

(6) Seth Eby married the second time, in 1850 Anna Schlott, widow of Samuel Schlott, and daughter of Christian and Martha Sherk, of West Hempfield township, Lancaster Co., Pa.

(6) Joel Eby was born March 19th, 1821. Died April 18th, 1880, aged 59 years and 29 days. He married in the year 1842,

Esther Hess, daughter of Henry and Catharine Hess.

(6) Joel and Esther (Hess) Eby begat children, viz:

(7) Maria H. Eby, married Michael Hostetter. Their children are, (8) Anna E. Hostetter, (8) Maria E. Hostetter, (8) Susan E. Hostetter, (8) Catharine E. Hostetter, (8) Ella E. Hostetter, (8) Levi E. Hostetter.

(7) Catharine H. Eby married John Huber.

(7) Fannie H. Eby, (7) Lizzie H. Eby, (7) Henry H. Eby.

(5) Benjamin Eby (Preacher) was born October 5th, 1797. He died in Franklin Co., Pa., April 16th, 1866, aged 68 years, 6 months and 11 days. He married February 18th, 1823, Veronica Wittwer, daughter of Jonas and Veronica Wittwer. She was born August 5th, 1798.

(5) Benjamin and Veronica (Wittwer) Eby begat children, viz:

(6) Jonas W. Eby, born November 26th, 1823. He married Susan Hershey, daughter of Preacher Jacob and Anna Hershey. Their children are, (7) Benjamin H. Eby, (7) Reuben H. Eby married to Amanda Reiff, (7) Amanda H. Eby, (7) Susan H. Eby, (7) Noah H. Eby, (7) Fannie H. Eby, (7) Jonas H. Eby, (7) Mary H. Eby.

(6) Christian W. Eby (Deacon), born June 19th, 1826. He married Martha Hershey, daughter of Preacher Jacob and Anna Hershey. Their children are, (7) Elam H. Eby, married to Lizzie Reiff, (7) Fannie H. Eby, married to Jacob Martin, (7) Mattie H. Eby, (7) Amon H. Eby, (7) John H. Eby.

(6) Christian W. Eby married the second time.

(6) Sem W. Eby, born February 10th, 1829. Died August 22d, 1832, aged 3 years, 6 months and 12 days.

(6) Veronica W. Eby, born September 28th, 1832. She married Jacob Risser (Preacher), son of Preacher John and Elisabeth Risser. Their children are, (7) John E. Risser, married to Barbara Martin, (7) Martin E. Risser, (7) Susan E. Risser, married to Henry Keener, (7) Benjamin E. Risser, (7) Samuel E. Risser, (7) Mary E. Risser, (7) Mattie E. Risser, (7) Amos E. Risser.

(6) Benjamin W. Eby, born March 30th, 1835. He died March 15th, 1868, aged 32 years, 11 months and 16 days. He married —— Reiff. Their children are, (7) Anna Eby.

(6) Isaac W. Eby, born April 13th, 1838. He married Maria Martin, daughter of —— and —— Martin. Their children are, (7)

Jacob Martin Eby, (7) Fannie Ada Eby, (7) Amos Franklin Eby, (7) Lizzie May Eby, (7) Isaac Victor Eby.

(6) Henry W. Eby, born October 9th, 1840. Died September 28th, 1852, aged 11 years, 11 months and 19 days.

The above family of Pre. Benjamin Eby live nearly all in Maryland.

(5) Christian Eby was born January 1st, 1800. He died June 22d, 1855, aged 55 years, 5 months and 21 days. He married Elisabeth Kreider, widow of Jacob Kreider, and daughter of Jonas and Susan (Wittwer) Bucher. She was born August 10th, 1806, and died June 11th, 1875, aged 68 years, 10 months and 1 day.

(5) Christian and Elisabeth Eby begat children, viz:

(6) Lizzie Eby, married to Abraham Rohrer. Their children are, (7) Mary E. Rohrer, (7) Amos E. Rohrer, (7) Lizzie E. Rohrer, (7) Anna E. Rohrer, (7) Daniel E. Rohrer, (7) Fannie E. Rohrer, (7) Noah E. Rohrer, (7) Ira E. Rohrer.

(6) Anna Eby married, to John E. Gingrich. (This family is described in the " Gingrich" family.)

(5) Barbara Eby was born October 4th, 1802. She married Abraham Reist, Decem-

ber 10th, 1822. He was born August 23d, 1798, and died September 23d, 1844, aged 46 years and 1 month.

(5) Abraham and Barbara (Eby) Reist begat children, viz :

(6) Aaron E. Reist, born May 29th, 1827. He married in 1854 Anna Zug. Their children are, (7) Nathan Elman Reist, (7) Aaron Edmund Reist.

(6) Moses E. Reist, born July 21st, 1829. He died May 5th, 1883, aged 53 years, 9 months and 14 days.

(6) Elias E. Reist, born November 22d, 1831. He married, in 1855, Catharine Keller.

(6) Benjamin E. Reist, born May 11th, 1834. He married, in 1864, Rebecca Gochenauer. Their children are, (7) Menno G. Reist, (7) Ellen G. Reist, (7) John G. Reist, (7) Benjamin G. Reist.

(6) Sybilla E. Reist, born January 3d, 1837. She married, in 1856, Preacher Benjamin Eby. Their children are, (7) Lizzie R. Eby, (7) Anna R. Eby, (7) Sybilla R. Eby, (7) Maria R. Eby, (7) Barbara R. Eby.

(6) Maria E. Reist, born December 29th, 1839. Married, in 1859, Samuel Oberholtzer. Their children are, (7) Anna R. Oberholtzer, (7) Menno R. Oberholtzer, (7) Nathan R. Oberholtzer.

(6) Esther E. Reist, born September 24th, 1842. Married, in 1865, Abraham Rutt. Their children are, (7) Aaron R. Rutt, (7) Cyrus R. Rutt, (7) Abraham R. Rutt.

(5) Susan Eby was born March 4th, 1805. She died April 27th, 1882, aged 77 years, 1 month and 23 days, she married Henry Stauffer. (Described in the "Stauffer" family.)

(5) Sem Eby was born May 4th, 1808. He died May 7th, 1881, aged 73 years and 3 days. He married, in the year 1831, Anna Frantz, daughter of Jacob Frantz. Anna Frantz was born November 22d, 1810, and died —— ——.

(5) Sem and Anna (Frantz) Eby lived in Leacock township, Lancaster Co. They begat children, viz:

(6) Jacob F. Eby, married to Hetty Rohrer. Their children are, (7) Lizzie A., (7) Mary E., (7) Amos R.

(6) Lizzie F. Eby.

(6) Elias Eby, married to Mary Ann Buckwalter. Their children are, (7) Enos B., (7) Anna V., (7) Milton B., (7) Harry S.

(6) Benjamin F. Eby married to Hettie Buckwalter. Their children are, (7) Ira M., (7) Amaziah B., (7) Ada E., (7) Aldus F.,

(6) Benjamin F. Eby married the second time Lizzie Hoover. Their children are,

(7) Anna S., (7) Harry F., (7) Lena B., (7) Sem H., (7) Hetty A., (7) Susan E., (7) Amos B., (7) Naomi.

(6) Christian F. Eby, died single.

(6) Sem F. Eby, married to Susan Eby. Their children are, (7) Walter H., (7) Clara A.

(6) Amos F. Eby married to Anna McKillips. Their children are, (7) Laura M.

(6) Ezra F. Eby, (6) Henry F. Eby, (6) Joseph M. Eby.

(6) John H. Eby, married to Lizzie Mellinger. Their children are, (7) Anna M., (7) Sem., (7) Mary E., (7) John M.

RETURN NOW TO PETER EBY (BISHOP.)

(4) Peter Eby (Bishop) was born October 14th, 1765. He died April 6th, 1843, aged 77 years, 5 months and 23 days. He married, in July, 1788, Margarette Hess, daughter of —— ——. Margarette Hess was born October 7th, 1764, died February 14th, 1845, aged 80 years, 4 months and 7 days.

(4) Peter and Margarette (Hess) Eby begat children, viz:

(5) Peter Eby, married to Elisabeth Weaver. Their children are,

(6) Elias Eby, married to Elisabeth Worst, and Clarissa Wilson. Their chil-

dren are, (7)Emma, (7)Elisabeth, (7)Rachel, (7) Henry Clay, (7) John Douglas, (7) Sarah, (7) Peter, (7) Richard.

(6) Susan Eby married to Isaac Worst. Their children are, (7) Lucinda, (7) Elisabeth, (7) David, (7) Margarette (7) George, (7) Eby, (7) Isaac Taylor, (7) Henry.

(6) Jacob Eby, married to Magdalena Wanner. Their children are, (7) Elias W., (7) C. Clement, (7) Peter W., (7) Elisabeth, (7) Margarette, (7) Mary, (7) Isaac, (7) Franklin, (7) Ella, (7) Jacob.

(6) Margarette Eby, married to Jacob R. Hershey (Preacher). Their children are, (7) Josiah, (7) Magdalena, (7) Ephraim, (7) Peter, (7) Mary, (7) Jacob, (7) Susan.

(6) Josiah Eby married to Ann W. Gondor.

(6) Elisabeth Eby, married to Abner Buckwalter. Their children are, (7) Ella, (7) Amer, (7) Justus, (7) Franklin.

(6) Henry W. Eby, single.

(6) Peter Eby, married to Martha Eckert. Their children are, (7) Henry, (7) Elisabeth, (7) Annie, (7) Franklin, (7) Jacob, (7) Ira.

(6) Isaac Eby (Bishop), married to Mary Mellinger. Their children are, (7) John M., (7) Peter, (7) Anna M., (7) Elisabeth, (7) Susan, (7) Henry B., (7) Mary, (7) Martha

Emma, (7) Magdalena, (7) Isaac W., (7) Esther.

(5) Susan Eby, married to David Hoover. Their children are,

(6) Mary Hoover, married to Isaac Moyer. Their children are, (7) David H., (7) Isaac.

(6) Henry Hoover, married to Catharine Longenecker. Their children are, (7) Susan, (7) one died.

(6) Anna Hoover, single.

(6) Margarette Hoover, married to John Hershey. Their children are, (7) David, (7) Susan.

(6) David Hoover, married to Sarah Carpenter.

(6) Abraham Hoover, married to Mary Carpenter. Their children are, (7) Ellen, (7) Margarette, (7) Martha, (7) Juliet, (7) Catharine, (7) John.

(5) Christian Eby, married to Rebecca Wittwer. Their children are,

(6) Maria Eby, married to Henry Breckbill. Their children are, (7) Amaziah E., (7) Naomi Ada, (7) Elmira Clara, (7) Susan Rebecca, (7) Preston E, (7) Seymore Henry.

(6) Margarette Eby, single.
(6) Elisabeth Eby, single.
(6) David Eby, single.

(6) Levi Eby, married to Susan Harnish. Their children are, (7) Elias H., (7) Mary A., (7) Annie E., (7) Rebecca E.

(6) Rebecca Eby, married to Henry Rohrer. Their children are, (7) Salmon Clasa, (7) John Henry, (7) Elsie V. Elisabeth.

(6) Samuel Eby, married to Mary Ann Esbenshade. Their children are, (7) Kezia, (7) Phares, (7) Elisabeth Ann.

(6) Benjamin Eby, married to Anna Buckwalter. Their children are, (7) Christian B., (7) Barbara, (7) Hettie A., (7) Salome, (7) Rufus, (7) Laura, (7) Lizzie, (7) Benjamin F., (7) Susan L., (7) Harry B., (7) Alice.

(6) Catharine Eby, married to Emanuel Neff. Their children are, (7) Rebecca Ann, (7) Enos, (7) Harry E., (7) Christian, (7) John, (7) Mary, (7) Catharine.

(6) Emanuel Eby, married to Ann Groff.

(5) Barbara Eby, married to John Stauffer. Their children are,

(6) Benjamin Stauffer, married to Catharine ——. Their children are, (7) Hettie, (7) John, (7) Abraham, (7) Henry, (7) Barbara, (7) Emma, (7) Amos, (7) Eliza, (7) Frank.

(6) Fannie Stauffer, married to Henry Landis. Their children are, (7) Anna, (7) Barbara, (7) Margarette, (7) Susan, (7)

Amos, (7) John, (7) Maria, (7) Henry, (7) Emma, (7) Emanuel, (7) Fremont, (7) Reuben.

(6) Peter Stauffer, married to Magdalena Bushong. Their children are, (7) John, (7) Amos, (7) Jacob.

(6) Christian Stauffer, married to —— Rohrer. Their children are, (7) John. (6) Christian Stauffer married the second time to Susan Root. Their children are, (7) Henry, (7) Christian, (7) Barbara, (7) Susan, (7) Benjamin.

(6) John Stauffer, married to Catharine Bressler. Their children are, (7) Isaac, (7) Freeland, (7) Mary.

(6) Margarette Stauffer, married to Henry Bressler. Their children are, (7) Lizzie, (7) Isaac, (7) John, (7) Henry, (7) Mark, (7) Emma, (7) Frank, (7) Delila.

(6) Anna Stauffer, married to John R. Hess (Preacher). Their children are, (7) John, (7) Amos, (7) Simon, (7) Daniel, (7) Abraham, (7) Benjamin, (7) Lizzie, (7) Anna, (7) Maria.

(6) Barbara Stauffer, married to Isaac Heller. Their children are, (7) Lizzie, (7) Annie, (7) John.

(5) Anna Eby, married to Abraham Hershey. Their children are,

(6) Margarette Hershey, married to Daniel Denlinger. Their children are, (7) Abraham, (7) Anna, (7) Mary, (7) Hettie, (7) Elisabeth, (7) Daniel H., (7) Margarette.

(6) Peter E. Hershey, married to Anna Landis. Their children are, (7) Christian, (7) Anna, (7) Henry, (7) Mary, (7) Landis.

(5) John Eby, married to Anna Rupp. Their children are,

(6) Barbara Eby, married to Abraham Hershey. Their children are, (7) Lydia, (7) Barbara, (7) Emanuel R., (7) Susan, (7) Henry, (7) Christian S., (7) Magdalena, (7) Abraham.

(6) Peter Eby, married to Elisabeth Kurtz. Their children are, (7) Anna, (7) Elisabeth.

(6) Christian Eby, married to Margarette Diller. Their children are, (7) Anna, (7) Amanda, (7) Isaac, (7) John.

(6) John Eby, married to Caroline Weaver.

(6) Henry Eby, married to —— Souders. Their children are, (7) John, (7) Dora.

(6) Anna Eby, married to James Skiles. Had one child. The father died; the widow married again to —— Miller. Had four children. Could not ascertain their names.

(5) Henry Eby, married to Susan Sensenig. Their children are,

(6) Peter Eby, married to Magdalena Musser. Their children are, (7) Susan, (7) John, (7) Elisabeth, (7) Magdalena, (7) Mary.

(6) John Eby, single.

(6) Margarette Eby, married to Jacob Musser. Their children are, (7) Henry E., (7) John. The father died. The widow married again to David Weaver. Their children are, (7) Franklin, (7) David.

(6) Susan Eby, married to Abraham Metzler. Their children are, (7) Christian, (7) Anna, (7) Henry, (7) Susan, (7) Abraham, (7) Isaac.

(6) Henry Eby, married to Barbara Herr. Their children are, (7) Abraham, (7) Anna.

(6) Elisabeth, Eby married to John Kenaegy. Their children are, (7) Henry, (7) Emanuel, (7) John.

(6) Joseph Eby, married to Susan Martin. Their children are, (7) Martin, (7) Samuel.

(6) Jacob Eby, married to Susan Ranck. Their children are, (7) John, (7) Jacob, (7) Annie, (7) Susan, (7) Hannah, (7) Mary, (7) Henry, (7) Margarette.

(6) Jonas Eby, married to Mary Denlinger. Their chiidren are, (7) Daniel, (7) Susan, (7) Ephraim, (7) Margarette, (7) Walter, (7) Emanuel.

(5) Elisabeth Eby, married to Jacob Hershey (Preacher). Their children are,

(6) Margarette Hershey, married to John B. Mellinger. Their children are, (7) Anna, (7) Elisabeth, (7) Elias, (7) Josiah, (7) Susan.

(6) John E. Hershey, married to Anna Mellinger. Their children are, (7) Jacob M., (7) Isaac E., (7) Anna, (7) Benjamin, (7) John, (7) Mary, (7) Susan

(6) Elisabeth Hershey, married to Jacob Mellinger. Their children are, (7) Margarette, (7) John, (7) Ezra, (7) Anna. (7) Jacob, (7) Frances.

(6) Elias Hershey, married to Anna Kreider. Their children are, (7) John, (7) Elisabeth, (7) Susan, (7) David E., (7) Sabina.

(6) Peter Hershey, married to Barbara Buckwalter. Their children are, (7) Sarah, (7) Esaias, (7) Enos, (7) Lizzie, (7) Henry, (7) Martha, (7) Martin, (7) Barbara, (7) Silas.

(6) J. Menno Hershey, married to Mary Harsh. Their children are, (7) Hannah Elisabeth, (7) Samuel Tilden.

(5) Maria Eby, married to Daniel Wanner. Their children are,

(6) Magdalena Wanner, married to Joseph Oberholtzer. Their children are, (7) Maria, (7) Daniel, (7) Abraham, (7) Joseph, (7) Susan, (7) Catharine, (7) Martin.

(6) Margarette Wanner, married to Henry Wenger. Their children are, (7) Samuel, (7) Elisabeth, (7) Susan, (7) Daniel, (7) Henry, (7) Abraham, (7) David, (7) Magdalena, (7) Mary, (7) Margarette.

(6) Daniel Wanner, married to Sarah Sensenig. Their children are, (7) Daniel, (7) Margarette, (7) Amos, (7) Elisabeth, (7) Maria, (7) Henry, (7) Anna, (7) Susan, (7) Samuel, (7) Ida.

(6) Maria Wanner, married to Moses Weaver. Their children are, (7) Alice, (7) Samuel, (7) Moses, (7) Benjamin, (7) Martha, 7) Henry.

(6) Samuel Wanner, married to Fianna Matzall. Their children are, (7) John, (7) Samuel, (7) Daniel, (7) Aaron.

(6) Catharine Wanner, married to Joseph Oberholtzer. Their children are, (7) David, (7) Peter, (7) Anna, (7) Magdalena, (7) Margaretta, (7) Lydia.

(6) Anna Wanner, married to Peter Souder. Their children are, (7) Maria, (7) Alice, (7) Anna, (7) Moses, (7) Emma, (7) Barton, (7) Susan, (7) Margarette.

(6) Susan Wanner, married to Edwin Gehr. Their children are, (7) Samuel, (7) Celia, (7) John.

(6) John Wanner, married to Mary Ann

Gehman. Their children are, (7) Mary, (7) Sarah, (7) Samuel.

RETURN AGAIN TO JOHN EBY.

(4) John Eby was born October 23d, 1767. He died May 25th, 1845, aged 77 years, 7 months and 2 days. He married July 1st, 1794, Mary Wittwer, daughter of Michael and —— (Sensenich) Wittwer, born August 25th, 1773. Died August 29th, 1856, aged 83 years and 4 days. Her brothers and sisters names are, Jonas Wittwer, married to Veronica Reiff. Hulda Wittwer, married to Stauffer. Magdalena Wittwer, single.

(5) John and Maria (Wittwer) Eby lived in Elisabeth twp., Lancaster Co. They begat children, viz:

(5) Catharine Eby, married to John Hostetter, son of John and Magdalena (Resh) Hostetter. Their children are,

(6) Magdalena Hostetter, married to Henry Shenk. Their children are, (7) Levi (Preacher), (7) John, (7) Mary, (7) Anna, (7) Sarah, (7) Henry.

(6) Mary Hostetter, married to Christian Herr. Their children are, (7) Fanny, (7) Christian, (7) Susan, (7) Anna, (7) Mary.

(6) Catharine Hostetter, married to Ja-

cob Shenk. Their children are, (7) Henry, (7) Amos, (7) Fannie, (7) Catharine.

(6) Henry Hostetter, died single.

(6) Elias Hostetter, married to Mary Ann Lehman.

(6) Jonas E. Hostetter, married to Barbara K. Nissly. Their children are, (7) Tillman, (7) Jacob, (7) Levi, (7) Mary, (7) Abner, (7) Amos, (7) Elam, (7) Jonas, (7) Simon.

(6) Abraham Hostetter, married to Rose Hogendobler. Their children are, (7) Alice, (7) Fannie.

(6) John E. Hostetter, married to Elisabeth Stehman. Their children are, (7) Anna, (7) Lizzie, (7) Mary, (7) John, (7) Jonas, (7) Amos, (7) Ella, (7) Katie.

(5) Jonas Eby was born March 14th, 1799. He married, December 12th, 1819, Veronica (Nissly) Huber, widow of Abraham Huber. They had one daughter, Anna, married to John Bassler and Daniel Kreider. She was a daughter of Bishop Samuel Nissly, of Rapho twp., Lancaster Co. She was born June 21st, 1798, and died October 30th, 1839, aged 41 years, 4 months and 9 days.

(5) Jonas and Veronica (Nissly) Eby, begat children, viz:

(6) John N. Eby, born 1820, married to

Charlotte Becker, daughter of John and Elisabeth (Keihl) Becker. Their children are, (7) Jonas (7) Charlotte, (7) one died small. (6) John N. Eby, married the second time, to Matilda Huber, daughter of George and Veronica (Bucher) Huber. Their children are, (7) Zenas, (7) John, (7) Aldus, (7) Fanny.

(6) Fanny N. Eby was born June 10th, 1823. She died January 10th, 1846, aged 22 years and 7 months. She was married to Martin B. Peiffer, of East Hempfield twp., Lancaster Co.

(6) Elias Eby, born February 8th, 1826. He married Martha Nissly, daughter of Jacob and Elisabeth (Krabill) Nissly. Her brothers and sisters are, Jacob K. Nissly, married to Anna E. Risser, Christian K. Nissly, Amos K. Nissly, Barbara K. Nissly, married to Jonas E. Hostetter, Maria K. Nissly, Kate K. Nissly, married to Michael Engle, Elisabeth K. Nissly, married to —— ——, Samuel K. Nissly, Ann K. Nissly, married to —— ——, Rebecca K. Nissly, married Jacob S. Mumma, Simon K. Nissly, married to Susan Elisabeth Hershey.

(6) Elias and Martha (Nissly) Eby's children are,

(7) Ephraim N. Eby, married to Amelia

Erb. Their children are, (8) Ephraim, (8) Elmer, (8) Emma, (8) Mary Ellen.

(7) Lizzie N. Eby, married Andrew G. Miller. Their children are, (8) Jonas, (8) Simon.

(7) Fanny N. Eby, married to Henry E. Garber. Their children are, (8) Tillman, (8) Ellen, (8) Jonas.

(7) Samuel N. Eby, married to Susan M. Garber.

(7) Reuben N. Eby, (7) Martha N. Eby, (7) Elias N. Eby, (7) Ellen N. Eby.

(6) Samuel N. Eby was born April 14th, 1828. He married Maria (Stauffer) Nissly, daughter of John and Elisabeth (Hostetter) Stauffer, of Petersburg, Lancaster Co., Pa. Her parents and brothers and sisters are described in the "Stauffer" family.

(6) Simon J. Eby, was born June 6th, 1831. He married in 1856, Catharine S. Lintner, daughter of Christian and Eliza Lintner, of Lancaster twp., Lancaster Co.

(6) Simon J. and Catharine (Lintner) Eby's children are, (7) Clinton L. Eby, born January 27th, 1858, died September 3d, 1861, aged 3 years, 7 months and 6 days. (7) Christian Lintner Eby, born June 16th, 1859, married Sadie Zellers, (7) Anna Elisabeth Eby, born July 27th, 1860. Mar-

ried Franklin Snavely, (7) Clayton S. Eby, born September 17th, 1862.

(6) Amos N. Eby, was born February 8th, 1835. He died February 9th, 1860, aged 25 years and 1 day.

(6) Henry N. Eby, was born August 16th, 1837. He married, in 1860, Mary S. Frank, (born in 1840 and died January 3d, 1876, aged 35 years, 7 months and 16 days), daughter of Christian and Catharine (Snyder) Frank, of Warwick twp., Lancaster Co. Her brothers and sisters are described in the "Reist" family.

(6) Henry N. and Mary S. (Frank) Eby's children are, (7) Daniel F. Eby, born April 9th, 1862, died October 8th, 1871, aged 9 years, 5 months and 29 days, (7) Amos F. Eby, born October 4th, 1864, (7) Fannie F. Eby, born May 31st, 1866, (7) Jonas F. Eby, born January 3d, 1869, died September 2d, 1869, aged 7 months and 30 days, (7) Levi F. Eby, born May 13th, 1870, (7) Anna Mary Eby, born March 5th, 1873.

(6) Henry N. Eby, married the second time in 1877, to Elisabeth Hostetter, daughter of David and Maria (Peiffer) Hostetter. She was born in 1841. Her brothers and sisters are mentioned in the "Hershey" family.

(6) Henry N. and Elisabeth (Hostetter) Eby's children are, (7) Elisabeth H. and (7)

Henry H. Eby, born November 19th, 1878, (7) David H. Eby, born July 14th, 1880.

(5) Mary Eby was born May 31st, 1801. She married Jacob Yundt, of Elisabeth twp., Lancaster Co., Pa. Their children are,

(6) John Yundt, (6) Allen Yundt, (6) Levi Yundt, (6) Rebecca Yundt, (6) Polly Yundt, (6) Samuel Yundt, (6) Jacob Yundt. This family moved to Illinois.

(5) Rebecca Eby was born December 3d, 1803. She married John Bomberger. (This family is described in the "Nissly" family.)

(5) Elias Eby was born February 21st, 1806. He died September 11th, 1862, aged 56 years, 6 months and 20 days. He was married to Elisabeth Erb, daughter of Jacob and Elisabeth (Becker) Erb, born June 19th, 1807. Died August 15th, 1855, aged 48 years, 1 month and 27 days.

Jacob Erb was born March 7th, 1781, died July 10th, 1864, aged 83 years, 4 months and 3 days. Elisabeth (Becker) Erb was born May 14th, 1782, died July 5th 1812, aged 30 years, 1 month and 20 days. Jacob Erb was a son of Christian and Ann (Bomberger) Erb. Elisabeth (Becker) Erb was a daughter of Christian and —— (Brubacher) Becker.

(5) Elias and Elisabeth (Erb) Eby's children are,

(6) Simon P. Eby, born August 1st, 1827. He married, December 23d, 1862, Amelia F. Mengel, daughter of Henry and Hannah (Shaner) Mengel, of Berks Co., Pa.

(6) Simon P. and Amelia F. (Mengel) Eby begat one son, (7) John Henry Eby, born December 4th, 1872.

(6) Mary E. Eby was born April 5th, 1834. She married John Longenecker, of Lebanon Co., Pa. Their children are, (7) Alice E. Longenecker, married to Isaac Bowman, (7) William Heister Longenecker, (7) Jennie Longenecker, married to —— Snoke, (7) Ralph Longenecker.

(6) Eliza Ann Eby was born October 12th, 1846, died October 3d, 1878, aged 31 years, 11 months and 21 days.

(5) Elias Eby married the second time to Sarah Ann Myers, widow of Allen Summy.

(5) Elisabeth Eby was born October 16th, 1808. She died January 3d, 1876, aged 67 years, 2 months and 17 days. She married in 1827, Samuel Risser, son of Preacher Christian and Catharine Risser, of Warwick twp., Lancaster Co., Pa. His brothers and sisters are, Christian, born 1799, Preacher John born 1801, Anna, born 1805,

Henry born 1809. Samuel Risser died October 6th, 1850, aged ——.

(5) Samuel and Elisabeth (Eby) Risser's children are,

(6) Anna E. Risser, born June 1st, 1828. She married Jacob K. Nissly, son of Jacob and Elisabeth (Kraybill) Nissly, of East Donegal twp., Lancaster Co. His brothers and sisters are mentioned in the "Eby" family.

(6) Jacob K. and Anna E. (Risser) Nissly's children are,

(7) Ellen R. Nissly, born September 3d, 1851. She married Jonas S. Mumma, son of Jonas and Catharine (Sherk) Mumma.

(7) Jonas S. and Ellen R. (Nissly) Mumma's children are, (8) Franklin N. Mumma, born June 1st, 188–, (8) Lizzie N. Mumma, born January 2d, 1873, (8) Hallie N. Mumma, born December 14th, 1874. She died December 14th, 1881, aged 7 years, (8) Ellen Ruth Mumma, born August 1st, 1876.

(7) Elisabeth R. Nissly was born September 29th, 1856. She married Henry S. Hoffman, son of Christian and Anna (Snyder) Hoffman.

(7) Henry S. and Elisabeth R. (Nissly) Hoffman's children are, (8) Mary N. Hoffman, born April 9th, 1877, (8) Jacob N. Hoffman, born April 27th, 1881.

(7) Matilda R. Nissly was born December 1st, 1858. She died August 11th, 1882, aged 23 years, 8 months and 10 days. She married Joseph Habecker.

(7) Joseph and Matilda R. (Nissly) Habecker's children are, (8) Anna N. Habecker, born July 14th, 1878, (8) Bessie N. Habecker, born January 3d, 1881.

(6) Mary E. Risser, was born August 4th, 1831. She died May 21st, 1857, aged 25 years, 9 months and 17 days. She married in 1855, John M. Baer.

(6) Levi E. Risser was born April 19th, 1834. He died July 17th, 1857, aged 23 years, 2 months and 28 days.

(6) Jonas E. Risser was born September 20th, 1837. He married, in 18—, Lizzie Hershey, daughter of Benjamin and Catharine Hershey, of Manor twp., Lancaster Co., Pa.

(6) Jonas E. and Lizzie Risser's children are, (7) David H. Risser, (7) Anna H. Risser.

(6) Reuben E. Risser was born June 29th, 1840. He married, in 1865, Sarah Hershey, daughter of Isaac and Anna Hershey, of East Donegal twp., Lancaster Co.

(6) Reuben E. and Sarah Risser's children are, (7) Horace, (7) Philip, (7) Edith. This family lives in Nebraska.

(6) Samuel W. Risser was born November 16th, 1843. He died January 15th, 1869, aged 25 years, 1 month and 29 days. He married, in 1866, Frances Kraybill, daughter of John N. and Fannie Kraybill, of West Donegal twp., Lancaster Co., Pa.

(6) Samuel W. and Frances (Kraybill) Risser's children are, (7) Margie, (7) Susan.

(6) Joseph E. Risser was born September 25th, 1846. He died July 13th, 1869, aged 22 years, 9 months and 18 days.

The mother of the above family, Lizzie (Eby) Risser, married the second time to Pre. Peter Risser, son of Jacob and Maria (Snyder) Risser, of Mount Joy twp., Lancaster Co., Pa. Pre. Peter Risser died June 21st, 1864, aged 66 years, 10 months and 2 days. His brothers and sisters are, Pre. John Risser, married to Barbara Huber, and Elisabeth Risser, married to John Hess.

(5) Levi Eby was born December 31st, 1810. He died April 17th, 1860, aged 49 years, 3 months and 17 days. He married, in 1837, Anna (Nissly) Gerber, widow of Andrew Gerber, and daughter of Pre. John and Anna (Hershey) Nissly, of Rapho twp., Lancaster Co., Pa. She was born August 6th, 1810. Died May 1st, 1866, aged 55 years, 8 months and 26 days. Her brothers and sisters are mentioned in the "Nissly" family.

(5) Levi and Anna (Nissly) Eby, begat children viz:

(6) Mary N. Eby was born December 3d, 1837. She married, in 1857, Christian S. Nissly, son of Dea. John and Barbara (Snyder) Nissly, of Mount Joy twp., Lancaster Co. His brothers and sisters are, Dea. Henry S. Nissly. married to Anna B. Reist. (This family is mentioned in the "Reist" family.) Mary S. Nissly, married to Martin W. Nissly. (This family is mentioned in the "Nissly" family.

Fannie S. Nissly married to Christian K. Hostetter. Their children are, Henry, Lavina.

Sarah S. Nissly, John S. Nissly (mentioned elsewhere.)

Barbara S. Nissly, married to Samuel Gerber. Their children are, Ezra, Lizzie, Fannie, Sadie, Ira, Harry, Mary, John.

(6) Christian S. and Mary N. (Eby) Nissly begat children, viz:

(7) Reuben E. Nissly, married to Anna Wohlgemuth. Their children are, (8) Minnie.

(7) Fianna E. Nissly married to Eli G. Reist (mentioned in the "Reist" family).

(7) John E. Nissly, (7) Phares E. Nissly, (7) Christian E. Nissly, (7) Milton E. Niss-

ly, (7) Franklin E. Nissly, (7) Tillie E. Nissly.

(6) A son born March 17th, 1839. Lived only eight days.

(6) Sarah N. Eby was born March 10th, 1841. She married John S. Nissly, son of Deacon John and Barbara (Snyder) Nissly.

(6) John S. and Sarah N. (Eby) Nissly begat children, viz:

(7) Charlotte E. Nissly, married to John B. Hertzler. Their children are, (8) Bertha N. Hertzler.

(7) Emma E. Nissly married to Benjamin M. Baer, (7) Phares E. Nissly, (7) Franklin E. Nissly, (7) Amelia E. Nissly, (7) Sarah E. Nissly, (7) Mary E. Nissly.

(6) Fianna N. Eby was born August 25th, 1846. She married John G. Snyder, son of Christian W. and Mary (Gerber) Snyder, of West Donegal township, Lancaster Co., Pa. His brothers and sisters are, Henry G. Snyder, married to Anna Bomberger, Christian G. Snyder, married to Sue Flory, Anna G. Snyder, married to Christian N. Newcomer.

(6) John G. and Fianna (Eby) Snyder's children are, (7) Levi E. Snyder, (7) Frances E. Snyder, (7) Emma E. Snyder, (7) Christian E. Snyder, (7) Anna E. Snyder.

(6) Fannie N. Eby (Described in the "Nissly" family).

(6) Rebecca N. Eby (Described in the "Nissly" family).

(5) Anna Eby was born January 28th, 1815. She died May 20th, 1879, aged 64 years, 3 months and 22 days. She married, in 1834, Samuel Hershey (Preacher), son of Christian and Elisabeth (Snyder) Hershey, of Penn township, Lancaster Co., Pa. His brothers and sisters are, Anna Hershey, married to Preacher John Nissly; Christian Hershey, married to Susan Baer; Barbara Hershey married to —— ——; Elisabeth Hershey, married to Henry Nissly; John Hershey, married to Barbara Reist; Isaac Hershey, married to Anna Martin and —— Nagle; Joseph Hershey died single; Maria Hershey, married to Samuel Nissly.

(5) Preacher Samuel and Anna (Eby) Hershey begat children, viz:

(6) Levi E. Hershsy, married to Catharine Buckwalter. Their children are, (7) John B. Hershey.

(6) Mary E. Hershey, married to Martin Hess. Their children are, (7) Reuben.

(6) Henry E. Hershey, married to Martha Brubacher. Their children are, (7) Samuel, (7) Lizzie, (7) Menno, (7) Anna, (7) Henry, (7) Mary, (7) Sarah.

(6) Anna E. Hershey, married to Jacob Becker. Their children are, (7) John, (7) Jacob

(4) Andrew Eby was born October 27th, 1769. He married Elisabeth Stauffer, daughter of Jacob and Elisabeth Stauffer. Her brothers and sisters are, Catharine Stauffer, married to Michael Weber. Their children are, Anna, Susan, Mary, Lydia, Jacob, Michael. Anna Stauffer married to Joseph Ebersole. Their children are, Jacob ——. Susan Stauffer, married to Samuel Bauman. Their children are, Leah, Elisabeth, Susan. Judith Stauffer, married to —— ——.

(4) Andrew and Elisabeth (Stauffer) Eby begat children, viz:

(5) Jacob Eby, married to Sallie Boyer. Their children are, (6) Amos, (6) Jacob, (6) Lizzie, (6) Sarah, (6) Anna. (6) Susan, (6) John, (6) Samuel.

(5) Catharine Eby, married to George Fry. Their children are, (6) David. (5) Catharine Eby married the second time, John Cover. Their children are, (6) Polly, (6) Mattie, (6) Israel, (6) Abraham, (6) Susan.

(5) Amos Eby, married to Catharine Plasterer Their children are, (6) Henry, (6) Lizzie, (6) Samuel.

(5) Mary Eby, married to John Gerber. Their children are, (6) Henry, (6) Samuel, (6) John, (6) Abraham, (6) Anna, (6) Andrew.

(5) Lizzie Eby, married to Abraham Behm. Their children are, (6) John, (6) Lizzie, (6) Abraham (6) Jacob, (6) Catharine, (6) Anna, (6) Elias.

(5) Anna Eby, married to George Geib.

(4) Andrew Eby (the father of the above family), died. His widow married the second time, Abraham Shiffer. Their children are, Susan Shiffer, married to Peter Tschudy; Abraham Shiffer married to Fianna Felker.

(4) Catharine Eby was born October 30th, 1771. She died March 4th, 1856. aged 84 years, 4 months and 5 days. She married June 26th, 1792. Abraham Burkholder son of Bishop Christian and Anna Burkholder, Earl township. Lancaster Co., Pa. This Christian Burkholder came, with his mother (a widow), three brothers and one sister, from Germany to America in the year 1755. He was born in Germany, June 1st, 1746. and died May 13th, 1809, aged 62 years, 11 months and 12 days. His wife's maiden name was Anna Groff. She died October 11th, 1795.

Abraham Burkholder, son of Bishop

Christian and Anna Burkholder, was born November 27th, 1768. He died January 15th, 1840, aged 71 years, 1 month and 18 days.

(4) Abraham and Catharine (Eby) Burkholder begat children, viz:

(5) Christian Burkholder, born May 22d, 1793. He died September 11th, 1872, aged 79 years, 3 months and 19 days. He married Veronica Groff. Their children are,

(6) Seth Burkholder, married to Magdalena Groff.

(6) Christian Burkholder, married to John B. Sensenig.

(6) Elias Burkholder, married to Maria Blair.

(6) Ezra Burkholder Esq., married to Magdalena A. Hoffman.

(6) Menno Burkholder, married to Barbara Hoover.

(6) Catharine Burkholder, married to John H. Martin.

(6) Maria Burkholder, married to Henry Meckley.

(6) Fannie Burkholder, married to Adam Moyer.

(6) Anna Burkholder, died single.

(6) Groff Burkholder.

(6) Christian Burkholder, died single.

(6) Peter Burkholder, married to Magdalena Keller.

(5) Catharine Burkholder, married first to Peter Wanner, and the second time to Joseph Wenger. Their children are, (6) Abraham Wanner, (6) Elisabeth Wanner, (6) Mary Wanner, (6) Fannie Wanner, (6) Peter Wanner, (6) John Wenger, (6) Joseph Wenger.

(5) Abraham Burkholder, married to Fannie Stauffer. Their children are, (6) Israel Burkholder, (6) Mary Ann Burkholder, (6) Fannie Burkholder.

(5) Jonas Burkholder, married to Catharine Sauder. Their children are, (6) Susan Burkholder, (6) Isaac Burkholder, (6) Jacob Burkholder, (6) Samuel Burkholder, (6) Elisabeth Burkholder, (6) Joseph Burkholder, (6) Catharine Burkholder, (6) Mary Burkholder.

(5) Anna Burkholder, married to Jonas Nolt. Their children are, (6) Jonas Nolt, (6) Magdalena Nolt, (6) Catharine Nolt (6) Polly Nolt, (6) Elisabeth Nolt, (6) Anna Nolt, (6) Susan Nolt, (6) Lydia Nolt, (6) Benjamin Nolt, (6) Menno Nolt, (6) Sarah Nolt.

(5) John Burkholder married to Esther Sauder. Their children are, (6) Levi Burkholder, (6) Daniel Burkholder, (6)

David Burkholder, (6) Nancy Burkholder, (6) Hettie Burkholder. The father married the second time, Fannie Wenger. Their children are, (6) Abraham Burkholder, (6) Elisabeth Burkholder.

(5) Mary Burkholder, single.

(5) Susan Burkholder, married to Abraham Martin. Their children are, (6) Catharine Martin.

(5) Samuel Burkholder, died March 25th, 1858.

(4) Barbara Eby, born April 29th, 1774. She died March 13th, 1843, aged 68 years, 10 months and 14 days. She married, February 21st, 1798, Joseph Snyder, of Canada West. He was born May 24th, 1772, and died October 27th, 1843, aged 71 years, 5 months and 3 days.

(4) Joseph and Barbara (Eby) Snyder begat children, viz:

(5) Catharine E. Snyder, married to Joseph Shantz. Their children are,

(6) Veronica Shantz, married to Joseph Weaver.

(6) Simon Shantz, married to Judith Stauffer.

(6) Moses Shantz, married to Susanna Snyder.

(6) Barbara Shantz, married to Moses Springer.

(6) Maria Shantz, married to Isaac Shantz.
(6) Joseph Shantz, married to Catharine Martin.
(6) Menno Shantz, married to Elisabeth Snyder.
(5) Jacob E. Snyder, married to Elisabeth Clemmens. Their children are,
(6) Maria Snyder, died young.
(6) Moses Snyder, married to Hannah Shantz.
(6) Magdalena Snyder, married to Isaac H. Bauman.
(6) Barbara Snyder, married to Isaac Cressman.
(6) Leah Snyder, died young.
(6) Joseph C. Snyder, married to Elisabeth Betzner.
(6) Elisabeth Snyder, married to Isaac Cressman.
(6) Lydia Snyder, married to Jacob S. Betzner.
(6) Sarah Snyder.
(6) Jacob Snyder, died young.
(6) Franklin Snyder.
(5) Elisabeth E. Snyder, married to Jacob S. Shoemaker. Their children are,
(6) Barbara Shoemaker, married to Henry Huber.
(6) John Shoemaker, married to Fanny Huber.

(6) Mary Ann Shoemaker, married to John McNally.
(6) Magdalena Shoemaker, married to Joel Clemmens.
(6) Elisabeth Shoemaker.
(6) Joseph Shoemaker, died young.
(6) Isaac Shoemaker, died young.
(6) Hannah Shoemaker, married to Casper Hett.
(6) Jacob S. Shoemaker, married to Eliza Hall.
(6) Isabella Shoemaker, died young.
(6) Simon Shoemaker, died young.
(5) Veronica E. Snyder, married to Daniel Martin. Their children are,
(6) Anna Martin, married to Samuel Weaver.
(6) Levi Martin, married to Mary Lichty.
(6) Isaac Martin, died young.
(6) Barbara Martin, married to Benjamin L. Eby.
(6) Joseph Martin, married to Susan Lichty.
(6) Veronica Martin.
(6) Daniel Martin, married to Magdalena Eby.
(6) Tillman Martin, married to Nancy Martin.
(6) Mary Martin, married to Daniel Cressman.

(6) Judith Martin, married to Menno Weidman.

(5) Mary E. Snyder, married to Christopher Nahrgang. Their children are,

(6) Joseph Nahrgang, married to Mary Shantz.

(6) Elisabeth Nahrgang, married to Benjamin D. Shantz.

(6) John Nahrgang, married to Mary Shantz.

(6) Barbara Nahrgang, married to Aaron Shantz.

(6) Isaac Nahrgang, married to Catharine Bricker.

(6) Mary Nahrgang, married to Daniel Shantz.

(6) Isabella Nahrgang, married to Amos Shantz.

(6) Simon Nahrgang, married to Lizzie Smith.

(5) Joseph E. Snyder (Deacon), married to Sarah Shantz. Their children are,

(6) Isaac Snyder, died young.

(6) Barbara Snyder, married to Abraham Hagey.

(6) David Snyder, married to Elisabeth Bricker and Sarah Meyer.

(6) Samuel Snyder, married to Rebecca Fried.

(6) Mary Snyder, married to David Bricker.
(6) Louisa Snyder, married to John Troxel.
(6) Lydia Snyder, married to John Fervier.
(6) Magdalena Snyder married to Nathan Bergy.
(6) Sarah Snyder, married to David Thaler.
(6) Hannah Snyder, married to Aaron Shantz.
(5) Moses E. Snyder, married to Molly Clemmens. Their children are,
(6) Barbara Snyder, married to Noah Betzner.
(6) Ezra Snyder, married to Lucinda Shantz.
(6) Magdalena Snyder, married to John Snyder.
(6) Levi Snyder, married to Mary Betzner, and Magdalena Hiestand.
(6) Isaac Snyder, married to Mary Ann Shantz.
(6) Mary Ann Snyder.
(6) Ephraim Snyder, married to Margarette Culp.
(6) Noah Snyder, (6) Moses Snyder, (6) Hannah Snyder, (6) Lucinda Snyder.
(4) Anna Eby was born September 9th,

1777. She died April —, 1829, aged 51 years and 7 months. She married Jacob Wissler, of Clay township, Lancaster Co., Pa. He died in 1852, in his 77th year.

(4) Jacob and Anna (Eby) Wissler begat children, viz:

(5) Andrew Wissler, married to Sarah Sherk. Their children are, (6) Andrew, (6) Jacob, (6) Elias, (6) Anna, (6) Maria, (6) Lucy, (6) Sarah.

(5) Jacob Wissler, described in the "Nissly" family.

(5) Christian Wissler, married to Anna Hostetter. Their children are, (6) Elisabeth, (6) Benjamin, (6) Jacob, (6) Mary Ann.

(5) Magdalena Wissler, married to Jacob Landis. Their children are, (6) Jacob, (6) Ezra, (6) Eliza, (6) Mary Ann.

(5) Ezra Wissler, married to Mary Bowman. Their children are, (6) Aaron B., (6) John B.

(5) John Wissler, married to Hannah Heiser. Their children are, (6) Franklin, (6) Jacob, (6) Levi, (6) Aaron, (6) Hannah, (6) Angelia.

(5) Catharine Wissler, died single.

(5) Mary Wissler, married to Levi Erb. Their children are, (6) Mary Ann, (6) Lizzie.

(5) Levi Wissler, married to Fanny Hess. Their children are, (6) John, (6) Levi, (6) Jacob, (6) Samuel, (6) Anna, (6) Barbara, (6) Fannie, (6) Mary, (6) Hannah.

(5) Samuel Wissler, married to Jane Robinson. Their children are, (6) John, (6) Ezra, (6) Levi, (6) Samuel, (6) Mary, (6) ——.

(4) George Eby, was born September 30th, 1779. Died in his 14th year.

(4) Maria Eby was born November 4th, 1781. Died April 9th, 1783, aged 1 year, 5 months and 5 days.

(4) Benjamin Eby (Bishop) was born May 2d, 1785, died June 28th, 1853, aged 68 years, 1 month and 26 days. He married February 25th, 1807, Maria Brubacher, daughter of Jacob and Susan (Erb) Brubacher, of Elisabeth township, Lancaster Co. Maria Brubacher was born August 6th, 1789, died August 18th, 1834, aged 45 years and 12 days.

(4) Benjamin and Maria (Brubacher) Eby, moved to Canada West, in the year 1807. He was ordained to the ministry, November 27th, 1809. He was ordained as Bishop, October 11th, 1812.

(4) Benjamin and Maria (Brubacher) Eby begat children, viz:

(5) Isaac Eby, born July 30th, 1808. He married, in 1831, Veronica Shoemaker,

daughter of John and Mary (Shantz) Shoemaker. Her brothers and sisters are, Jacob, married to Elisabeth Snyder; Isaac; John, married to Veronica Seiler; Barbara, married to John Roat; Mary, married to Michael Meyers; Joseph; Magdalena, married to Barnabas Dewitt; David, married first to Margarette Nickerbocker, and as his second wife, to Louisa Nickerbocker.

(5) Isaac and Veronica (Shoemaker) Eby, begat children, viz :

(6) Menno Eby, married to Mary Elisabeth S. Becker. Their children are, (7) Eve Magdalena, (7) Sophia Maria, (7) Louisa Matilda, (7) Alexander, (7) Ida Isabella, (7) Leander, (7) Menno, (7) Nellie Grace.

(6) Mary Eby, married to Abraham Groff. Their children are, (7) Susan, (7) Levi, (7) Leah, (7) Ezra, (7) Maria, (7) Lydia Ann, (7) Matilda, (7) Isaac Eby, (7) Hannah, (7) Emma, (7) Abraham, (7) Benjamin, (7) Jacob.

(6) Isaac S. Eby, married to Elisabeth Stauffer. Their children are, (7) Maria, (7) Veronica, (7) Harriet, (7) Isaiah, (7) Martha, (7) Angelia, (7) Lizzie, (7) Leander, (7) Jemima, (7) Benjamin.

(6) Daniel Eby, married Frances Myers. Their children are, (7) Emma Zelena, (7) Asa Theophilus, (7) Effa Zilpha.

(6) Christian Eby, married to Catharine Clemmens. Their children are, (7) Lydia Ann, (7) James Edward, (7) Isabella, (7) Jacob, (7) Foster

(6) Theodore Eby, married to Susan Reist.

(6) Barnabas Eby.

(6) Ezra E. Eby, married to Mary Ann Clemmer. Their children are, (7) Ira, (7) Odo, (7) Ion, (7) Leo.

(6) Benjamin S. Eby, married to Helen Zeigler.

(6) Lydia Ann Eby.

(5) Elias Eby was born February 22d, 1810, died June 1st, 1878, aged 68 years, 3 months and 9 days. He married, in 1834, Anna Weaver, daughter of Benjamin and Veronica (Martin) Weaver. Her brothers and sisters are mentioned in the "Brubacher" family.

(5) Elias and Anna (Weaver) Eby begat children, viz :

(6) Josiah Eby.

(6) Mary Eby.

(6) Benjamin W. Eby, married to Hannah Kraft. Their children are, (7) Norman, (7) Lydia Ann, (7) Albert, (7) Laura.

(6) Magdalena Eby, married to Isaac E. Shantz. Their children are, (7) Josiah, (7) Tillman, (7) Edmund, (7) Elmira, (7) Mary Ann, (7) Milton.

(6) Veronica Eby, married to Aaron E. Shantz. Their children are, (7) Nettie, (7) Malinda, (7) Jacob, (7) Adaline, (7) Edwin, (7) Ida, (7) Elsie, (7) Edith.

(6) Anna Eby, married to Benjamin Reesor. Their children are, (7) Harvey, (7) Walter, (7) Fannie.

(6) Elias W. Eby, (6) Tobias Eby, (6) Christian Eby. (6) Moses Eby.

(5) Susan Eby was born February 8th, 1812, died in 1819.

(5) Catharine Eby was born July 25th, 1814. She married, in 1833 David Weaver, son of Benjamin and Veronica (Martin) Weaver. His brothers and sisters are mentioned in the "Brubacher" family.

(5) David and Catharine (Eby) Weaver begat children, viz :

(6) Elias Weaver, married to Mary Shoemaker. Their children are, (7) Sarah, (7) Simon, (7) Lavina, (7) Leah, (7) Anna, (7) Lydia, (7) Amos, (7) Israel, (7) Maria.

(6) Susan Weaver, married to John Schun. Their children are, (7) Franklin, (7) Levi.

(6) Andrew Weaver, married to Veronica Shantz. Their children are, (7) Melissa, (7) Ellen, (7) Sabina, (7) Ephraim, (7) Manassa, (7) Elsie, (7) Edwin, (7) Ivan.

(6) Mary Weaver, married to Moses De-

witt. Their children are, (7) Albert, (7) Edwin, (7) Malinda, (7) Melissa, (7) Noah, (7) Mary.

(6) Peter E. Weaver, married to Magdalena Clemmens.

(6) Magdalena Weaver, married to Amos Weaver. Their children are, (7) Mary Ann, (7) Ida, (7) Allen, (7) Lucinda, (7) Menno, (7) Solomon.

(6) Veronica Weaver, married to Jacob Kinsie. Their children are, (7) Elam, (7) Rosetta, (7) Isaiah, (7) Agabus, (7) Luanna.

(6) Theodore Weaver, married to Sarah Woolner. Their children are, (7) Susanna, (7) Simon, (7) Celina, (7) Hannah.

(6) Henry Weaver, married to Anna Zeller. Their children are, (7) Ada Cecilia.

(6) Lucinda Weaver, married to Eli C. Shantz. Their children are, (7) Velina.

(6) Matilda Weaver, married to Casper Smith. Their children are, (7) Harvey, (7) Milton.

(5) Maria Eby was born March 14th, 1816. She married, in 1840, William Bomberger, son of Christian and Mary (Erb) Bomberger. His brothers and sisters are, Emanuel, Maria, John, Christopher, Jacob.

(5) Benjamin Eby was born February 10th, 1818. He married, in 1842, Elisabeth Cressman, daughter of Abraham and Mary

(Snyder) Cressman. Her brothers and sisters are, Daniel, married to Anna Eby and Veronica Eby ; Samuel, married to Barbara Cressman ; Joseph ; Mary, married to Preacher Christian Eby ; Jacob, married to Susan Snyder ; Esther : Abram, married to Susan Snyder and Mary Wissmer ; John, married to Mary Shantz ; Isaac, married to Barbara Snyder and Elisabeth Snyder ; Amos, married to Anna Martin ; Nancy, married to Daniel Bowman.

(5) Benjamin and Elisabeth (Cressman) Eby begat children, viz :

(6) Mary Eby, married to John Erb. Their children are, (7) Angeline, (7) Sarah.

(6) Amos Eby, married to Hettie Moyer. Their children are, (7) Allan, (7) Louisa, (7) Matilda, (7) Norman, (7) Josiah, (7) Ida.

(6) Leah Eby, married to Moses Kinsie. Their children are, (7) Simon, (7) Lavina.

(6) Sarah Eby, married to David Moyer. Their children are, (7) Lucinda, (7) Urias, (7) Lizzie, (7) Adaline, (7) Phoebe, (7) Ida, (7) Sarah.

(6) Susan Eby, died young.

(5) Henry Eby was born January 25th, 1820. He married, in 1843, Elisabeth Bowers, daughter of Samuel and Lydia (Sowers) Bowers. Her brothers and sisters are, Harriet, married to Robert Barber ; Louisa,

married to Gabriel Bowman ; Isaac W., married to Jane Camp ; William, married to Mary Ann Collins ; Jacob S., married to Elisabeth Quickfall ; Levi, married to —— —— ; Samuel, married to Jane Flowers ; Lavina, married to David Kilborn ; Mary Ann, married to Jacob W. Bowman.

(5) Henry and Elisabeth (Bowers) Eby begat children viz :

(6) Julia Ann Eby, married to Richard C. Cowan. Their children are, (7) Robert Henry, (7) William Craig, (7) Charles Edward, (7) Walter Richard, (7) Thomas Albert, (7) Maria Louisa, (7) Richard Eby, (7) Frederick Harold, (7) Alice Olga.

(6) Harriet Eby, married to Isaac B. Burkholder. Their children are, (7) Arthur Henry, (7) Daniel Fairford, (7) Alfred, (7) Mary Alice.

(6) Adalaide Eby, married to Daniel C. Bowman.

(5) Preacher Christian Eby was born June 19th, 1821. He was ordained to the ministry in 1854. He died in 1859. He married, in 1843, Mary Cressman, daughter of Abraham and Mary (Snyder) Cressman. (Her brothers and sisters have been mentioned.)

(5) Christian and Mary (Cressman) Eby begat children, viz :

(6) Moses Eby, (6) Christian Eby—both children died young.

(5) Abraham Eby was born November 21st, 1823. He married, in 1843, Lucy Hembling, daughter of Noah and Hanna (Rose) Hembling. Her brothers and sisters are, William, married to Mary Derstein and Elisabeth Martin ; Jeremia, married to Susan Jones ; Elenor, married to Jacob Hoffman ; Mary; Jacob; Sarah; Rachel.

(5) Abraham and Lucy (Hembling) Eby begat children, viz :

(6) Hannah Eby, married to Jonas Detweiler. Their children are, (7) Louisa, (7) Lucy Ann, (7) Adelaide, (7) Mary, (7) Irwin, (7) Hannah, (7) Magdalena.

(6) Magdalena Eby, married to John Auman. Their children are, (7) Edward, (7) Lucy, (7) Henry, (7) Ida, (7) Charlotte, (7) Oscar, (7) Angeline.

(6) Tillman Eby.

(6) Phoebe Eby, married to Henry Lachman. Their children are, (7) Lucy Etta, (7) Charles, (7) Mary Ann, (7) Albert, (7) Isaac, (7) Leah, (7) William.

(6) Herman Eby, married to Mary Ann Heiseman. Their children are, (7) Lillie, (7) Allan, (7) Adalaide, (7) Estella, (7) Hermenia.

(6) Edward Eby.

(6) Noah Eby, married to Susan Hilborn. Their children are, (7) Abram, (7) Edward, (7) Charlotte.

(6) Charlotte Eby; (6) Dianna Eby; (6) William Eby, married to Susan Galer; (6) Isaac H. Eby.

(5) Jacob B. Eby was born March 24th, 1826. He married, in 1845, Lucy Kauffman, daughter of Andrew and Mary (Erb) Kauffman. Her brothers and sisters are, Solomon, married to Elisabeth Bauman and Mary Ann Groff; Allan, married to Hannah Zeigler; Urias; William; Joseph; Charles, married to —— ——; Polly, married to John Hohn and Elias B. Snyder; Nancy, married to Isaac C. Bowman; Caroline, married to John B. Knorr; Magdalena.

(5) Jacob B. and Lucy (Kauffman) Eby begat children, viz:

(6) Franklin Eby, married to Huldah Butler.

(6) Andrew Eby, married to Magdalena Soeder. Their children are, (7) Oscar, (7) Herbert.

(6) Amelia Eby, married to Hugh Streets. Their children are, (7) Lucy, (7) Franklin, (7) Mary, (7) Nancy, (7) Russel.

(6) Blandinah Eby, married to William

Bridon. Their children are, (7) Andrew, (7) Charles, (7) Agnes. (7) Maud.

(6) Magdalena Eby, married to Charles Findlay. Their children are, (7) Jacob, (7) Agnes, (7) Lloyd, (7) Stanley.

(6) Nancy Eby ; (6) Caroline Eby; (6) Urias Eby; (6) Henry Eby; (6) Daniel Eby; (6) Allan Eby; (6) Ida Eby ; (6) Emma Eby; (6) Jacob Eby.

(5) Jacob B. Eby married the second time, Elisabeth Schill, daughter of John and Anna Martha (Hildebrand) Schill. Her sister Anna Martha, married Adam Gottsleben.

(5) Jacob B. and Elisabeth (Schill) Eby begat children, viz:

(6) Jacob B. Eby.

(5) Peter Eby was born February 28th, 1828. He married, in 1848, Susan Sparrow, daughter of Thomas and Sarah (West) Sparrow. Her brothers and sisters are, Robert; John W.; Thomas W., married to Lydia Weethee; Mary Ann; Kezia W., married to William Prest; Caroline, married to Isaac Anderson; John Wesley, married to Libby Robinson.

(5) Peter and Susan (Sparrow) Eby begat children, viz:

(6) Isidore Emanuel Eby, married to Agnes A. Stoddard. Their children are,

(7) Mary Florence, (7) Lillie Margarette, (7) Albert Henry, (7) Catharine Norman. (Here ends the "Eby" family.)

RETURN AGAIN TO (4) JACOB BRUBACHER.

(4) Jacob and Maria (Eby) Brubacher begat children, viz:

(5) Susan Brubacher was born February 6th, 1808. She married, March 21st, 1826, Jacob Brubacher, son of Daniel and Elisabeth (Stauffer) Brubacher, of Lebanon Co., Pa. (His brothers and sisters are described in (2) Daniel Brubacher's family.)

(5) Jacob and Susan (Brubacher) Brubacher begat children, viz:

(6) Peter B. Brubacher, born in 1828. He married, in 1851, Elisabeth Landis, daughter of Christian and Mary Landis. Her brothers and sisters are,

Levi Landis, married to Mary Buckwalter. Their children are, Elam, Hettie, Amanda, Mary, Lydia, Emma.

Anna Landis, married to Peter Hershey. Their children are, Christian, Anna, Henry, Mary, Landis.

Catharine Landis, married to Preacher Christian Risser. Their children are, Reuben, Mary, Amos, Henry, Christian.

Pre. John L. Landis, married to Mary Denlinger. Their children are, Aaron.

Hettie Landis, married to Martin Herr. Their children are, Mary, Anna, Amanda, Lizzie, Hettie, Emma, Benjamin, Landis, Lydia.

(6) Peter B. and Elisabeth (Landis) Brubacher begat children, viz:

(7) Henry L. Brubacher, born January 8th, 1853. He married, in 1876, Anna Hess, daughter of Samuel and Fannie Hess. Her brothers and sisters are, Fannie, Henry, Fannie, Maria, Susan.

(7) Henry L. and Anna (Hess) Brubacher begat one child. It died young. The mother died in 1877.

(7) Henry L. Brubacher married the second time in 1881, Anna, daughter of John and Anna Stauffer,

(7) Henry L. and Anna (Stauffer) Brubacher begat children, viz: (8) Jacob S. Brubacher.

(7) Mary L. Brubacher, born May 16th, 1855. She married, in 1881, Isaac Landis, son of Henry L. and Catharine Landis. His brothers and sisters are, Andrew, Peter, Harry, Benjamin, Jacob, Israel, Anna, Lizzie, Catharine, Ellen, Clara.

(7) Anna L. Brubacher, born December 8th, 1860.

(6) Maria B. Brubacher, born in 1832. She married, in 1857, Amos Weaver, son of Jonathan and Anna Weaver. His brothers and sisters are,

Samuel Weaver, married to Anna Martin. Their children are, John, Mary, Anna, Barbara, Lizzie.

David Weaver, married to Lydia Wittmer. Their children are, Israel, Anna.

Martin Weaver, married to Barbara Reif. Their children are, Amanda, Aaron, Maria, Jonathan, Barbara.

Mary Weaver, married to John Sensenig. Their children are, Amos, Mary Ann.

Jonathan Weaver, married to Sarah Moyer. Their children are, Anna, Moyer, Hettie, Joseph, Barbara, David, Elam, Sarah.

Josiah Weaver, married to Mary Peifer. Their children are, Samuel, John.

Ezra Weaver, married to Lizzie Zimmerman. Their children are, Catharine, Amos, Anna, Jonathan, Mary, Jacob, Lydia.

Amos Weaver died in 1862. His widow, (6) Maria B. Weaver, married the second time in 1863, John Erb, son of Daniel and Mary Erb, of Penn township, Lancaster Co., Pa. His brothers and sisters are,

Elisabeth Erb, married to Christian B. Peifer. Their children are, Daniel, Mary, Martin, Lizzie.

Anna Erb, married to Benjamin Baer. Their children are, Adaline, Mary, Benjamin, Daniel, Lizzie.

Mary Erb, married to Jacob Brubacher, of Lancaster township, Lancaster Co., Pa. Their children are, Christian, Benjamin, Jacob, Samuel, Daniel, David, Maria, Susan.

David Erb, married to Catharine Groff. Their children are, Israel G., Maria, Adaline.

Daniel Erb, married to Susan Stauffer. Their children are, Mary, Harry, Anna Susan, Wellington S., Emma Frances, Tilly Agnes, Daniel S., Willes S

John Erb, died February 11th, 1872, aged 36 years, 10 months and 11 days.

(6) John B. Brubacher, born January 27th, 1836. He died, in 1853, in his 17th year.

(6) Elisabeth B. Brubacher, born January 18th, 1842. She died March 23d, 1871, aged 29 years, 2 months and 5 days. She married, in 1863, Christian Oberholtzer, son of Christian and Anna (Hess) Oberholtzer. His brothers and sisters are,

John Oberholtzer, married to Maria Groff. Their children are, Franklin, Mary, Susan, Emma.

Henry Oberholtzer, married to Lavina

Reist. Their children are, Henry, Florence, Ida May.

Hettie Oberholtzer.

Anna Oberholtzer, married to Henry Moyer. Their children are, Daniel, Anna, Alice.

(6) Christian and Elisabeth (Brubacher) Oberholtzer begat children, viz:

(7) Jacob B. Oberholtzer, born June 15th, 1864.

(7) Christian B. Oberholtzer, born September 3d, 186–.

(6) Christian Oberholtzer, married the second time, to Lydia Weaver, daughter of Frank and —— Weaver.

(6) Christian and Lydia (Weaver) Oberholtzer begat children, viz: Henry, Anna Mary.

(5) Mary Brubacher was born October 14th, 1809. She was married, in 1828, to John Reist, son of Christian and Barbara Reist, of Warwick township, Lancaster Co., Pa. John Reist was born March 16th, 1805, and died June 6th, 1877, aged 72 years, 2 months and 20 days. His brothers and sisters are,

Elisabeth Reist, married to Joseph Eby. Their children are, Anna, Eliza, Jacob, Joseph, Maria, Samuel.

Anna Reist, married to John Stehman. Their children are, Polly, Elisabeth, Fannie.

Barbara Reist, married to John Hershey. Their children are, one, died young.

Jacob Reist, died single.

(5) John and Mary (Brubacher) Reist begat children, viz:

(6) Anna B. Reist, born June 20th, 1829. She married, October 23d, 1849, Henry S. Nissly (Deacon), son of Deacon John and Barbara (Snyder) Nissly, of Mount Joy township, Lancaster Co., Pa.

Henry S. Nissly, born in 1827. His brothers and sisters are described in the "Eby" family.

(6) Henry S. and Anna B. (Reist) Nissly begat children, viz:

(7) Levi R. Nissly, born July 17th, 1850. He married, in 1871, Lizzie L. Nissly, daughter of Christian H. and Barbara (Lindemuth) Nissly, of Mount Joy township, Lancaster Co., Pa. His brothers and sisters are mentioned in the "Reist" family.

(7) Levi R. and Lizzie L. (Nissly) Nissly begat children, viz: (8) Henry, (8) Christian, (8) Lizzie, (8) Frances, (8) Katie.

(7) Fannie R. Nissly, born April 24th, 1852. Died January 27th, 1858, aged 5 years, 9 months and 3 days.

(7) Barbara R. Nissly, born June 9th, 1855. Died September 3d, 1855, aged 2 months and 24 days.

(7) Maria R. Nissly, born June 9th, 1855. Died March 27th, 1857, aged 1 year, 9 months and 18 days.

(7) Amos R. Nissly, born November 19th, 1857. He married, in 1883, Frances L. Baer, daughter of Samuel R. and Amelia (Lane) Baer. Her sister, Anna L. Baer, is married to Martin K. Brubacher, son of Jonas and Leah (Keller) Brubacher.

(7) Anna R. Nissly, born December 21st, 1859. She married, December 20th, 1878, Abraham L. Nissly, son of Jacob W. and Mary (Lindemuth) Nissly, of Mount Joy township, Lancaster Co., Pa. His brothers are, Clayton L. Nissly, married to Sarah R. Nissly ; Martin L. Nissly.

(7) Henry R. Nissly, born June 27th, 1863.

(7) Amanda R. Nissly, born July 20th, 1868.

(6) Henry B. Reist was born March 16th, 1832. He died March 14th, 1879, aged 46 years, 11 months and 27 days. He married, in October 1853, Catharine S. Gerber, daughter of John and Catharine (Siechrist) Gerber. Her brothers and sisters are,

Anna S. Gerber, married to John Longenecker (Deacon). Their children are, John, Levi, Katie, Anna, Christian, Lizzie, Mary.

Mary S. Gerber, married to Christian W.

Snyder. Their children are, John G., Henry G., Christian G.

John S. Gerber, married to Susan Erb. Their children are, Anna, Henry, Amos, John, Kate, Mary, Simon, Harriet, Samuel.

Christian S. Gerber, married to Anna Lindemuth. Their children are, Jacob, Mary, John, Christian, Katie, Barbara.

Fannie S. Gerber, married to David L. Miller. Their children are, John.

(6) Henry B. and Catharine (Gerber) Reist begat children, viz:

(7) Eli G. Reist, born March 9th, 1855. He married, in 1881, Fianna E. Nissly, daughter of Christian S. and Mary N. (Eby) Nissly. Her brothers and sisters are mentioned in the "Eby" family.

(7) Eli G. and Fianna E. (Nissly) Reist begat children, viz: (8) Lawrence.

(7) John G. Reist, born April 3d, 1857.

(7) Mary G. Reist, born August 11th, 1859. She married, in 1881, Samuel S. Krabill, son of Peter and Fannie (Snyder) Krabill. His brothers and sisters are mentioned in the "Nissly" family.

(7) Samuel S. and Mary G. (Reist) Krabill begat children, viz: (8) Ira.

(7) Henry G. Reist, born May 27th, 1862.
(7) Emma G. Reist, born April 4th, 1866.
(7) Anna G. Reist, born Jan. 8th, 1869.

(6) Christian B. Reist, born August 31st, 1834. He died February 24th, 1862, aged 27 years, 5 months and 21 days. He married, December 21st, 1861, Barbara Rutt, daughter of David and Magdalena Rutt, of Manor township, Lancaster Co., Pa. Her brothers and sisters are,

Elisabeth Rutt, married to Henry Huber. Their children are, Mary, Lizzie, Martha, Anna.

Jacob M. Rutt, married to Anna Kreider. They had one child, Anna.

Jacob M, Rutt, married the second time, Maria H. Brubacher. This family is mentioned in the "Brubacher" family.

David Rutt, married to Anna Kreider and Mary Kendiz. Their children are, Christian, Emma, Susan, Benjamin, Mary, David, Frances.

Martha Rutt, married to David E. Nissly. Their family is mentioned in the "Nissly" family.

Mary Ann Rutt, married to Abraham Newcomer. Their children are, Alice, Amos, Martha, Abraham, Mary, Ellen, Lizzie.

Christian M. Rutt, married to Lydia Kauffman and Susan Herr. Their children are, Ida, Edes.

(6) Christian B. Reist, died childless. His widow married Henry S. Stauffer.

(6) Maria B. Reist, born June 4th, 1837. She married in September, 1855, John K. Nissly, son of Preacher Peter and Catharine (Kreider) Nissly, of Donegal township, Lancaster Co., Pa. His brothers and sisters are,

Mary Nissly, married to Solomon Schwartz. Their children are, Maria, Anna.

Hettie Nissly, died single.

Leah Nissly, married to David L. Miller, Their children are, Anna, Barbara, Mary, Milton, Lizzie.

Barbara Nissly, married to Christian Hostetter. Their children are, Catharine.

Anna Nissly, died single.

Christian K. Nissly, died single.

Catharine Nissly, died single.

(6) John K. and Maria B. (Reist) Nissly begat children, viz:

(7) Sarah R. Nissly, born November 12th, 1856. She married, in 1875, Clayton L. Nissly, son of Jacob W. and Mary (Lindemuth) Nissly, of Mount Joy township, Lancaster Co., Pa. His brothers and sisters are mentioned elsewhere.

(7) Clayton L. and Sarah R. (Nissly) Nissly begat children, viz: (8) Bertha.

(7) Maria R. Nissly, born December 1st, 1859. Married to George R. Risser.

(7) Peter R. Nissly, born September 6th, 1863.

(7) Fannie R. Nissly, was born March 31st, 1867.

(6) Barbara B. Reist was born October 1st, 1839. She married, November 9th, 1858, Henry S. Snavely, (born November 21st, 1833), son of Henry and Mary Ann (Stauffer) Snavely, of Penn township, Lancaster Co. His sister, Mary Ann Snavely, married Martin N. Brubacher, described in the "Brubacher" family.

(6) Henry S. and Barbara B. (Reist) Snavely begat children, viz:

(7) Martin R. Snavely, born December 17th, 1859.

(7) Maria R. Snavely, born November 13th, 1861.

(7) Lizzie R. Snavely, born April 27th, 1863.

(7) Henry R. Snavely, born July 26th, 1865.

(7) Barbara R. Snavely, born January 31st, 1867.

(7) John R. Snavely, born March 26th, 1874. He died, December 25th, 1880, aged 6 years, 8 months and 29 days.

(6) John B. Reist was born April 16th,

1842. He married, October 25th, 1868, to Fannie S. Frank, daughter of Christian and Catharine (Snyder) Frank, of Warwick township, Lancaster Co., Pa. Her brothers and sisters are,

John Frank, married to Anna Hess. Their children are, Amos, Christian, Henry, John.

Henry Frank, married to Susan Hess. Their children are, Anna, Jonas, Henry.

Mary Frank, married to Henry N. Eby. (This family is mentioned in the "Eby" family.)

Anna Frank, married to Jonas Hess Their children are, Lizzie, Kate, Christian, Fannie, Henry, Jonas, Ellen, Anna.

Christian Frank, married to Mary Risser. Their children are, Ella, Lizzie, Emma, Ada, Mamie, Levi, Christian, Harry.

(6) John B. and Fannie S. (Frank) Reist begat children, viz:

(7) Katie F. Reist, born March 3d, 1873.
(7) Clara F. Reist, born August 6th, 1875.
(7) Anna F. Reist, born July 29th, 1879.
(7) Henry F. Reist, born Feb. 26th, 1881.
(7) John F. Reist born September 13th, 1883, died October 9th, aged 26 days.

(6) Jacob B. Reist was born September 18th, 1844. He married, November 16th, 1865, Mary E. Peifer, daughter of Christian B. and Elisabeth (Erb) Peifer, of East

Hempfield township, Lancaster Co., Pa. Her brothers and sisters are,

Daniel E. Peifer, married to Maria Huber. Their children are, Monroe, Phares, Lizzie, Henry.

Martin E. Peifer, married to Mary Ann Kreider. Their children are,

Lizzie E. Peifer, died single.

(6) Jacob B. and Mary E. (Peifer) Reist begat children, viz:

(7) Amelia P. Reist, born Nov.16th, 1867.

(7) Lizzie P. Reist, born Feb. 16th, 1869.

(7) Amos P. Reist, born January 25th, 1871, died April 21st, 1872, aged 1 year, 2 months and 26 days.

(7) Mary P. Reist, born Oct. 16th, 1872.

(7) Amanda P. Reist, born December 8th, 1874.

(7) Christian P. Reist, born October 22d, 1876, died, March 21st, 1877, aged 4 months and 30 days.

(7) Adaline P. Reist, born Dec. 3d, 1878.

(7) Emma P. Reist, born July 14th, 1880.

(7) Susan P. Reist, born Nov. 8th, 1882.

(6) Sarah B. Reist was born January 16th, 1847. She married, October 29th, 1867, Israel G. Erb, son of David W. and Catharine (Groff) Erb, of Penn township, Lancaster Co., Pa. His brothers and sisters are,

Maria Erb, married to Daniel Landis.

Their children are, Emma, David. Maria Erb, married the second time Christian W. Kreider. Their children are, Katie.

Adaline Erb, married to John Brubacher. Their children are, Wayne.

(6) Israel G. and Sarah B. (Reist) Erb begat children. viz :
(7) Emma R. Erb, born Oct. 27th, 1870.
(7) Mary R. Erb, born March 7th, 1874.
(7) Katie R. Erb, born July 5th, 1878.
(7) Minnie R. Erb, born June 20th, 1883.
(6) Samuel B. Reist was born April 20th, 1849, died, February 19th, 1852, aged 2 years, 7 months and 29 days.

(6) Catharine B. Reist was born December 3d, 1851. She married November 19th, 1871, Christian L. Nissly, son of Christian H. and Barbara (Lindemuth) Nissly, of Mount Joy township, Lancaster Co., Pa. His brothers and sisters are,

Mary L. Nissly, married to Jacob Hershey. Their children are, Amanda, Ephraim, Jacob, Isaac, Barbara, Christian.

Amanda L. Nissly, married to Henry Meckley. Their children are mentioned elsewhere.

Lizzie L. Nissly, married to Levi R. Nissly. Their family is mentioned elsewhere.

(6) Christian L. and Catharine B. (Reist) Nissly begat children, viz:

(7) Emma R. Nissly, born August 19th, 1872. Died, August 22d, 1875, aged 3 years and 3 days.

(7) Alman R. Nissly, born Feb. 7th, 1874.

(7) Martin R. Nissly, born June 3d, 1876.

(7) John Franklin Nissly, born December 26th, 1880.

(5) Catharine Brubacher was born February 22d, 1811. She died October 20th, 1855, aged 44 years, 10 months and 28 days. She married Benjamin Hershey, son of Preacher Benjamin and Veronica (Snyder) Hershey, of Penn township, Lancaster Co., Pa.

Benjamin Hershey was born October 26th, 1804, died October 4th, 1882, aged 77 years, 11 months and 8 days. His brothers and sisters are,

Anna Hershey, married to John Snavely. Mentioned in the "Snavely" family.

Preacher Jacob Hershey, married to Anna Reist, Elisabeth Reist and Barbara Zimmerman. Their children are,

John, married to —— Kraybill; Esther, married to Henry Hess; Susan, married to Jonas W. Eby; Eliza, married to Henry S. Stauffer; Jacob, married to Fanny Huber; Martha, married to Christian W. Eby (Deacon); Barbara, married to Jacob Erb; Peter, married to Anna Hess.

Maria Hershey, married to Christian Hernly, their children are,

Samuel; Fannie, married to John Geib; Martha, married to Henry Strickler; Susan; Polly, married to Benjamin Longenecker; Barbara, married to Joseph Gonnelly; Christian, married to Catharine Bucher; Benjamin, married to Eliza Erb; Anna; Catharine. married to Daniel B. Erb; Sarah, married to John Heller.

Catharine Hershey, married to Jacob Stauffer. Their children are,

Benjamin, married to Susan Erb; Peter, married to Anna N. Newcomer; Anna; Fannie, married to Christian W. Snyder; Joseph; Christian, married to Catharine Nissly; Mary; Jacob married to Elisabeth N. Newcomer; Abraham, married to Lizzie Kreider; Henry, married to Susan B. Harnish; John; Samuel, married to Susan E. Greider, of Ohio.

Veronica Hershey, married to Joseph Reist and Deacon Isaac Kauffman.

Barbara Hershey married to Jacob Ebersole. Their children are, Anna, married to Aaron Brenneman.

Joseph, married to Lizzie Heise.

(5) Benjamin and Catharine (Brubacher) Hershey, died childless.

(5) Sem Brubacher was born January 11th, 1813. He married, in 1834, Magdalena Nissly, eldest daughter of Martin and Anna (Bomberger) Nissly, of Rapho township, Lancaster Co., Pa.

Martin Nissly was born November 6th, 1788. He died June 24th. 1872, aged 83 years, 7 months and 18 days. He was a son of Bishop Samuel and Barbara (Greider) Nissly, of Rapho township, Lancaster Co., Pa. Bishop Samuel Nissly was born in 1761, and died August, 1838. He was a son of John Nissly, of Mount Joy township, Lancaster Co. His mother's maiden name was "Siechrist". His brothers and sisters are, Michael, Abraham, John, Jacob, Martin, Fannie. John Nissly was a son of Jacob Nissly, who emigrated to America from Germany and settled in Mount Joy township, Lancaster Co., Pa.

Bishop Samuel Nissly is the 3d generation in America. His wife, Barbara Greider, was a daughter of Martin Greider, of East Hempfield township, Lancaster Co., Pa. Her brothers and sisters cannot be fully traced up any more.

The following is a description of Barbara

Greider's (Bishop Samuel Nissly's wife), brothers and sister,

John Greider, married to Magdalena Hertzler. Their children are, Martin, married to —— Hostetter; Elizabeth, married to John Bruckart; John, married to Anna Hershey; Christian, married to Susan Miller and Elisabeth (Keihl) Becker; Michael, married to Ann Hogendobler; Jacob, married to Catharine Herr; Maria, married to Abraham Herr; Magdalena, married to Martin Funk; Jacob Greider; Daniel Greider; Michael Greider. One of her sisters was married to Abraham Hershey, of whom there are many descendants at present. Martin Greider, married to Elisabeth Weldy. Their children are, Martin Greider, married to Barbara Musser; Daniel Greider, married to —— Gerber; Christian Greider, married to Margarette Lindemuth; John Greider, single; Samuel Greider, single; Henry Greider, single; Barbara Greider, married to Samuel Johnson; Anna Greider, married to Michael Harnish; Jacob Greider, married to Anna Kauffman.

Bishop Samuel Nissly, was married three times. He had four sons with his first wife, Barbara Greider; two sons and one daughter with his second wife, Anna (Mumma) Greider, widow; and none with his third wife, Maria (Long) Hohn, widow.

THE FOLLOWING IS A DESCRIPTION OF THE FAMILY OF (3) BISHOP SAMUEL NISSLY.

(4) John Nissly (Preacher) was born December 9th, 1786. He died November 21st, 1847, aged 60 years, 11 months and 12 days. He was married to Anna Hershey, daughter of Christian and Elisabeth Hershey, of Penn township, Lancaster Co. Pa. She was born November 20th, 1787, and died February 2d, 1863, aged 75 years, 3 months and 1 day. Her brothers and sisters are mentioned elsewhere.

(4) Preacher John and Anna (Hershey) Nissly begat children, viz:

(5) Elisabeth Nissly, born December 12th, 1808. She married Christian Newcomer (Deacon), born June 8th, 1808, died Feb. 24th, 1884, aged 75 years, 8 months and 16 days. son of Christian and Barbara Newcomer, of Manor township, Lancaster Co. His brothers and sisters are, Jacob, John (Preacher), Elisabeth, Catharine, Barbara, Magdalena.

(5) Christian and Elisabeth (Nissly) Newcomer begat children, viz:

(6) Anna N. Newcomer, born June 17th,

1830. She married January 3d, 1854, Peter H. Stauffer, son of Jacob and Catharine (Hershey) Stauffer. Their children are, (7) Christian, (7) Levi, (7) Amos, (7) Lizzie.

(6) Mary N. Newcomer, born April 24th, 1832. She married, January 13th, 1853, John Forry, Sr. Their children are, (7) Christian, (7) Catharine, (7) Daniel, (7) Lizzie, (7) Amos, (7) Anna, (7) Mary, (7) Emma, (7) Isaac, (7) Harry.

(6) John N. Newcomer, born September 20th, 1833, died July, 1843, aged nearly 10 years.

(6) Jacob N. Newcomer, born July 20th, 1835. He married October 21st, 1858, Barbara Weidman, daughter of David and Elisabeth Weidman, of Penn township, Lancaster Co., Pa, Her brothers and sisters are mentioned in the "Snyder" family. Their children are, (7) Lizzie, (7) Amos, (7) David, (7) Fannie, (7) Alice, (7) Levi, (7) Jacob, (7) John, (7) Barbara, (7) Ezra.

(6) Barbara N. Newcomer, born March 12th, 1837. She married, November 22d, 1855, Christian Hostetter, son of Preacher Jacob and Anna Hostetter, of Rapho township, Lancaster Co., Pa. Their children are, (7) Anna, (7) Reuben, (7) Lizzie, (7) Christian, (7) David, (7) Barbara, (7) Mary, (7) Abraham, (7) Jacob.

(6) Elisabeth N. Newcomer, born February 8th, 1840. She married, May 2d, 1861, Jacob H. Stauffer, son of Jacob and Catharine Stauffer. Their children are, (7) Simon, (7) Anna, (7) Eli, (7) Lizzie, (7) Fannie.

(6) Catharine N. Newcomer, born September 19th, 1842. She married, October 30th, 1865, Joseph Krabill, son of Peter and —— Krabill, of Donegal township, Lancaster Co., Pa. Their children are, (7) Lizzie, (7) Mary, (7) Ellen, (7) Anna, (7) Bertha.

(6) Christian N. Newcomer, born December 8th, 1845. He married, October 3d, 1867, Anna Snyder, daughter of Christian W. and Mary Snyder, of Donegal township, Lancastsr Co., Pa. Their children are, (7) Norman, (7) Harry, (7) Lizzie, (7) Christian, (7) Catharine, (7) Samuel.

(5) Anna Nissly was born August 5th, 1810. She married Andrew Gerber, son of Jacob and Barbara (Miller) Gerber, of Donegal township, Lancaster Co., Pa. They had one daughter, Anna, married to John Hertzler. They live in Alabama. The father, Andrew Gerber, died. His widow married the second time, Levi Eby, son of John and Maria (Wittwer) Eby, of Warwick

township, Lancaster Co., Pa. This family is described elsewhere.

(5) Veronica Nissly was born February 27th, 1812. She married, March 17th, 1835, Christian Nolt, born August 14th, 1806, son of Christian and Anna (Eshleman) Nolt, of West Hempfield township, Lancaster Co., Pa. His brothers and sisters are, Benjamin, married to —— Hostetter; Maria, married to John Hershey; Jonas married to Lizzie Mumma and Elisabeth Shroeder; Nancy, single; Elisabeth, single; John, single; Jacob, married to Eliza Hoffman.

(5) Christian and Veronica (Nissly) Nolt begat children, viz:

(6) Anna Nolt, born January 15th, 1836, married to Samuel Hiestand. Their children are, (7) Cyrus, (7) Samuel, (7) Anna, (7) Fannie, (7) Christian.

(6) John Nolt, born October 4th, 1837.

(6) Elisabeth Nolt, born November 10th, 1839.

(6) Mary Nolt, born July 29th, 1844.

(6) Benjamin Nolt, born March 8th, 1842. He married Anna Hoffman, daughter of Henry and Elisabeth Hoffman. Their children are, (7) Lillie, (7) Christian, (7) Fannie, (7) Anna, (7) Harry, (7) Minnie, (7) Clayton.

(6) Christian Nolt, born July 4th, 1851.

He married Maria Brubacher, daughter of Jacob and Maria Brubacher. Their children are, (7) Phares, (7) Susan, (7) Jacob, (7) John.

(6) Sarah Nolt, born in 1849. She died in 1881, aged 32 years, 9 months and 8 days.

(6) Barbara Nolt, born August 18th, 1855. Lived only three days.

(5) Catharine Nissly was born September 23d, 1827. She married John Musser, son of Benjamin and Barbara Musser, of East Hempfield township, Lancaster Co., Pa. His brothers and sisters are mentioned elsewhere.

(5) John and Catharine (Nissly) Musser's family are mentioned in the "Nissly" family.

(5) John Nissly was born in 1819. He died in 1874, aged 54 years, 8 months and 20 days. He married Barbara Gerber, daughter of Jacob and Barbara (Miller) Gerber, of Donegal township, Lancaster Co., Pa. Her brothers and sisters are, Benjamin Gerber, married to Fianna Landis. Their children are, Israel; Barbara; Anna, married to Joseph Risser; Benjamin L., married to Caroline Weaver; Fianna, married to Clemen Brubacher; David L., married to Emma Hershey; Andrew Gerber, mentioned elsewhere.

(5) John and Barbara (Gerber) Nissly begat children, viz:

(6) Jacob G. Nissly, born April 5th, 1842. He married, in 1863, Catharine E. Stauffer, daughter of Henry and Susan (Eby) Stauffer, of Rapho township, Lancaster Co., Pa. This family is mentioned in the "Stauffer" family.

(6) Anna Nissly, born November 10th, 1844.

(6) John G. Nissly, born March 29th, 1848. He married Fannie Musser, daughter of Martin and —— Musser, of West Hempfield township, Lancaster Co., Pa. Their children are, (7) Martin, (7) Barbara, (7) Jacob.

(6) Benjamin G. Nissly, born August 16th, 1850. He died, May 26th, 1868, aged 17 years, 9 months and 10 days.

(6) Andrew G. Nissly, born February 28th, 1853. He married, in 1873, Barbara H. Bomberger, daughter of Preacher Christian and Catharine Bomberger. Their children are, (7) Christian, (7) Elmira, (7) Barbara, (7) Amos.

(6) Barbara G. Nissly, born July 7th, 1855. She married, in 1873, John Herr, son of David and —— Herr, of Manor township, Lancaster Co., Pa. Their chil-

dren are, (7) Anna, (7) Barbara, (7) Alice, (7) Mary.

(4) Martin Nissly was born November 6th, 1788. His family will be described elsewhere.

(4) Samuel Nissly was born June 24th, 1792. He died September 8th, 1868, aged 76 years, 2 months and 14 days. He married Anna Eby, daughter of Christian and Veronica Eby, of Elisabeth township, Lancaster Co., Pa. Her brothers and sisters are mentioned in the " Eby" family. Anna Eby was born January 6th, 1791, died May 5th, 1867, aged 76 years, 3 months and 29 days.

(4) Samuel and Anna (Eby) Nissly begat children, viz:

(5) Henry E. Nissly was born December 17th, 1814. He died September 28th, 1852, aged 37 years, 9 months and 11 days. He married, in 1835, Anna Hostetter, born August 7th, 1814, daughter of Christian and Catharine (Kreider) Hostetter, of East Donegal township, Lancaster Co., Pa. Her brothers and sisters are, John Hostetter; Michael Hostetter, married to Catharine Kauffman; Christian Hostetter, married to Catharine Frank; Benjamin Hostetter, married to Elisabeth Hiestand; Catharine Hostetter, married to Jacob Newcomer; Preach-

er Jacob Hostetter, married to Ann Stauffer.

(5) Henry E. and Anna (Hostetter) Nissly begat children, viz:

(6) Anna H. Nissly, born December 8th, 1836. She married Jonas Mumma, son of Jonas and Maria (Hershey) Mumma. Their children are, (7) Samuel, (7) Fannie, (7) Jonas, (7) Israel, (7) Amos, (7) John, (7) Anna.

(6) David H. Nissly, born August 25th, 1838. He died, July 5th, 1862, aged 33 years, 10 months and 11 days.

(6) Henry H. Nissly, born October 18th, 1840. He married Christiana Greiner. Their children are, (7) Henry.

(6) Samuel H. Nissly, born July 15th, 1842. He died March 18th, 1843, aged 8 months and 3 days.

(6) Catharine H. Nissly. born April 13th, 1844. She married Abraham M. Stauffer. Their children are, (7) Morris, (7) Abraham, (7) John, (7) Samuel, (7) Harry.

(6) Lavina H. Nissly, born April 18th, 1846. She married Noah Nissly. Their children are, (7) Anna, (7) Noah, (7) Naomi, (7) Joel, (7) Fannie, (7) Enos, (7) Lavina.

(6) Harriet H. Nissly, born February 9th, 1851. She married Austin H. Clay, of Illinois.

(6) John H. Nissly, born February 23d, 1853, died April 8th, 1853, aged 1 month and 15 days.

(5) Fannie E. Nissly was born June 10th, 1816. She died, November 7th, 1880, aged 64 years, 4 months and 27 days. She married, in 1837, Samuel Snyder, son of John and Anna (Hostetter) Snyder, of East Hempfield township, Lancaster Co., Pa. His brothers and sisters are, Catharine, married to Henry Stauffer; Jacob, married to Adaline Rohrer; John, married to —— Shollaw.

(5) Samuel and Fannie E. (Nissly) Snyder begat children, viz :

(6) Jonas N. Snyder, born October 24th, 1837. He died October 7th, 1868, aged 30 years, 11 months and 13 days.

(6) Samuel N. Snyder, born March 8th, 1839. He married, in 1866, Elisabeth Strickler, daughter of Abraham and Barbara Strickler, of Rapho township, Lancaster Co., Pa.

(6) Christian N. Snyder, born March 6th, 1841, died August 16th, 1841, aged 5 months and 10 days.

(6) Anna N. Snyder, born June 29th, 1842, died December 23d, 1877, aged 35 years, 5 months and 24 days.

(6) Catharine N. Snyder, born May 20th,

1845. She married Henry Buch, son of Jacob and —— Buch, of East Hempfield township, Lancaster Co., Pa. Their children are, (7) Fannie.

(6) Fannie N. Snyder. born July 24th, 1848, died October 20th, 1860, aged 12 years, 2 months and 27 days.

(6) Rudolph N. Snyder, born December 29th, 1850, died January 11th, 1851, aged 13 days.

(6) Sarah N. Snyder, born December 29th, 1850, died January 19th, 1851, aged 20 days.

(6) Lizzie N. Snyder, born November 29th, 1851. She married Peter Shelly, son of Peter and —— Shelly, of Rapho township, Lancaster Co., Pa.

(6) David N. Snyder, born —, 1857. He married, in 1881, Emma Rhoads. Their children are, (7) John, (7) Amos.

(5) Samuel E. Nissly was born December 25th, 1818. He married, in 1842, Anna K. Long, daughter of Abraham and Anna Long, of East Hempfield township, Lancaster Co., Pa. Anna Long was born November 7th, 1823, died November 15th, 1863, aged 40 years and 7 days. Her brothers and sisters are,

Abraham K. Long, married to Susan Huber.

Christian K. Long, married to Anna

Hiestand. Their children are, Mary, Matilda, Abraham, Lizzie, Christian.

John K. Long, married to Eliza Miller. Their children are, Harman, Fannie.

Susan K. Long, married to Jacob Hershey. Their children are, Washington, Abraham, Amelia, Benjamin, Webster.

Fannie K. Long, married to Jacob B. Landis. Their children are, Benjamin, Samuel, Jacob, Ellen.

Benjamin K. Long.

Maria K. Long, married to Abraham Perry. Their children are, Anna.

(5) Samuel E. and Anna K. (Long) Nissly begat children, viz :

(6) Harriet L. Nissly, born August 15th, 1843. She married, in 1865, Jacob P. Hostetter, son of David and Maria (Peifer) Hostetter, of Penn township, Lancaster Co., Pa. Their children are, (7) Clayton, (7) Ellen.

(6) Jonas L. Nissly, born March 21st, 1845. He married, in 1869, Fannie Charles, daughter of John and —— Charles. of Manor township, Lancaster Co., Pa. Their children are, (7) Amos, (7) John, (7) Susan, (7) Franklin.

(6) Abraham L. Nissly, born March 22d, 1847. He married, in 1872, Adaline Kendig, daughter of Christian and Polly Kendig, of Manor township, Lancaster Co., Pa.

Their children are, (7) Anna. Adaline Nissly, the mother, died July 28th, 1873, aged 22 years, 10 months and 11 days. Abraham L. Nissly, married the second time to Barbara Smith. Their children are, (7) Harry Hoyt, (7) Edward, (7) Walter Scott.

(6) Samuel L. Nissly, born June 19th, 1849. He married, in 1871, Ellen Hershey, daughter of Christian and Susan (Swarr) Hershey, of East Hempfield township, Lancaster Co., Pa. Their children are, (7) Phares, (7) Lizzie.

(6) Harman L. Nissly, born August 1st, 1851.

(6) Benjamin L. Nissly, born October 25th, 1853. He married, in 1875, Anna Hostetter, daughter of Christian and Barbara (Newcomer) Hostetter, of Rapho township, Lancaster Co., Pa. Their children are, (7) Lizzie,(7) Ellen.

(6) Franklin L. Nissly, born March 29th, 1856. He married, in 1881, Lillie H. Hoffman, daughter of Henry and Elisabeth (Hiestand) Hoffman, of East Hempfield township, Lancaster Co. Their children are, (7) Harry, (7) Eda.

(6) Ellen L. Nissly, born September 20th, 1858, died March 30th, 1865, aged 6 years, 6 months and 10 days.

(6) Henry Lincoln Nissly, born March 10th, 1861.

(6) John L. Nissly, born November 7th, 1863, died August 25th, 1864, aged 9 months and 18 days.

Anna (Long) Nissly, the mother of the above family died.

(5) Samuel E. Nissly married the second time, in 1865, Maria (Hershey) Landis (widow), daughter of John and Mary (Rohrer) Hershey, of Penn township, Lancaster Co. She had one daughter, viz: Lizzie Landis. Her sisters are, Eliza Hershey, married to Isaac Hershey, and Levi Forrey; Anna Hershey, married to John Ressler.

(5) Christian E. Nissly was born December 25th, 1818. He is a twin brother to Samuel E. Nissly. He was married, in 1845, to Fannie Brenneman, daughter of Henry and Eve Brenneman, of Rapho township, Lancaster Co. Her brothers and sisters are,

Jacob Brenneman, married to Magdalena Kendig. Their children are, Christian, Henry, Barbara.

Elisabeth Brenneman, married to John B. Hertzler. Their children are mentioned elsewhere.

John Brenneman, married to Fannie Freed and Mary (Miller) Stauffer (widow). Their children are, Henry, Kate, Samuel, Fannie, Benjamin, Christian.

Maria Brenneman, married to Adam Herr. Their children are, Henry, Fannie, John, Mary, Eliza, Benjamin.

Nancy Brenneman, died single.

Harry Brenneman, married to Sarah Kauffman.

Martin Brenneman, married to Lizzie Kauffman. Their children are, Henry, Samuel, Christian, Mary, Martin.

Isaac Brenneman, married to Leah Kauffman. Their children are, Simon, Leah, Henry, John, ——, Alice.

(5) Christian E. and Fannie (Brenneman) Nissly begat children, viz:

(6) Henry B. Nissly, born March 28th, 1846. He married, in 1869, Rebecca H. Brubacher. This family is described in the "Brubacher" family.

(6) Samuel B. Nissly, born June 30th, 1847. He married, in 1871, Emma H. Rohrer, daughter of John and Anna (Hammaker) Rohrer, of East Hempfield township, Lancaster Co. Their children are, (7) Phares, (7) Samuel, (7) Norman, (7) Anna May.

(6) Jonas B. Nissly, born January 31st, 1850. He married, in 1877, Susan Herr, daughter of Daniel and Catharine (Gamber'

Herr, of Penn township, Lancaster Co. Their children are, (7) Daniel, (7) Christian, (7) Jonas.

(6) Anna B. Nissly, born April 13th, 1852. She married, in 1873, John Stehman, son of John and Fannie (Snavely) Stehman. Their children are, (7) Emma, (7) Elam, (7) John, (7) Anna, (7) Fannie.

(6) Catharine B. Nissly, born December 2d, 1854. She married, in 1874, Daniel Forry, son of John and Mary (Newcomer) Forry, of Rapho township, Lancaster Co. Their children are, (7) John, (7) Simon, (7) Ella, (7) Daniel.

(6) Fannie B. Nissly, born May 13th, 185–. She married, in 1879, Amos Shelly, son of David and Susan (Herr) Shelly, of Rapho township, Lancaster Co. Their children are, one, died.

(6) David B. Nissly, born November 2d, 1860, died September 3d, 1861, aged 10 months and 1 day.

(6) Ellen B. Nissly and Emma B. Nissly, born November 26th, 1865.

(5) Jonas E. Nissly was born May 27th, 1821, died February 12th, 1848, aged 26 years, 8 months and 16 days.

(5) Benjamin E. Nissly was born December 17th, 1823, described in the "Stauffer" family.

(5) Catharine E. Nissly was born November 1st, 1826.

(5) David E. Nissly was born November 28th, 1829. He married, in 1865, Martha Rutt, (born April 22d, 1843), daughter of David and Magdalena Rutt, of Manor township, Lancaster Co. Her brothers and sisters are mentioned in the "Reist" family.

(5) David E. and Martha (Rutt) Nissly begat children, viz :

(6) Menno R. Nissly, born February 14th, 1867.

(6) Amos R. Nissly, born July 14th, 1868.

(6) Elisabeth R. Nissly, born May 13th, 1870.

(6) Martha R. Nissly, born july 27th, 1871.

(6) David R. Nissly, born September 13th, 1873.

(6) Simon R. Nissly, born January 31st, 1875.

(4) Christian Nissly (Preacher) was born October 20th, 1794. He died July 6th, 1882, aged 87 years, 7 months and 16 days. He was married to Magdalena Bomberger, daughter of Joseph and Magdalena Bomberger, of Warwick township, Lancaster Co. She was born, January 27th, 1799, died August 15th, 1869, aged 70 years, 6 months and 19 days. Her brothers and

sisters are described in the "Bomberger" family.

(4) Christian and Magdalena (Bomberger) Nissly begat children, viz:

(5) Magdalena B. Nissly was born May 6th, 1818. She married Andrew Gerber, son of Jacob and Barbara (Miller) Gerber, of East Donegal township, Lancaster Co. His brothers and sisters are mentioned elsewhere.

(5) Andrew and Magdalena B. (Nissly) Gerber, begat children, viz :

(6) Christian N. Gerber, born April 27th, 1837, married to Catharine Stoner. Their children are, (7) Martin S. Gerber, (7) Martha S. Gerber, (7) Sarah S. Gerber, (7) Benjamin S. Gerber, (7) Catharine S. Gerber, (7) Samuel S. Gerber, (7) Barbara S. Gerber, (7) Christian S. Gerber.

(6) Andrew N. Gerber, born December 18th, 1839, died December, 1843, aged 5 years and — days.

(5) Joseph B. Nissly, was born January 19th, 1821. He married, December 8th, 1842, Martha Sherk (born March 25th, 1824), daughter of Christian and Martha Sherk, of West Hempfield township, Lancaster Co. Her brothers and sisters are, John, married to —— Gochenauer and Lucinda Musselman ; Joseph, married to

Mary Greider ; Christian, married to Anna Gochenauer; Catharine, married to Jonas Mumma ; Maria, married to Preacher Peter Nissly ; Susan, married to Daniel Hoffman; Anna, married to Preacher Samnel Schlott and Seth Eby ; Lizzie, married to Christian Flory.

(5) Joseph B. and Martha (Sherk) Nissly, begat children, viz :

(6) Martha S. Nissly, born May 1st, 1845. She married Amos R. Strickler, son of John and Catharine (Rohrer) Strickler, of Rapho township, Lancaster Co. Their children are, (7) Elmer, (7) William, (7) Joseph, (7) Christian, (7) Anna, (7) Alice.

(6) Christian S. Nissly, born June 15th, 1847. He married Matilda H. Long, daughter of Christian K. and Anna (Hiestand) Long. Their children are, (7) Emma, (7) Lizzie, (7) Anna, (7) Christian.

(6) Samuel S. Nissly, born December 14th, 1848. He married Priscilla Zieger. Their children are, (7) Laura Ann, (7) Clayton.

(6) Joseph S. Nissly, born January 3d, 1851, married to Fianna Moore. Their children are, (7) Cyrus, (7) Alvin, (7) Ellen.

(6) Anna S. Nissly, born July 13th, 1854, died July 18th, 1879, aged 25 years and 5 days. She married Henry H. Shenk, son

of Henry and Magdalena (Hostetter) Shenk. Their children are, (7) Lizzie, (7) Anna.

(5) Martha (Sherk) Nissly, the mother of the above family died September 27th, 1859, aged 35 years, 6 months and 2 days.

(5) Joseph B. Nissly, married the second time, January 26th, 1871, to Elisabeth F. Wittmer (born May 16th, 1842), daughter of Peter and Elisabeth Wittmer. Her brothers and sisters are, Catharine, died single ; Jacob, married to Anna Krabill ; Peter, married to Elisabeth Strickler ; Jonas, married to Magdalena Hoffman ; Henry, married to Barbara Clark ; Anna, married to Jesse Moyer ; Fannie, married to Jacob Sauders ; Mary.

(5) Christian B. Nissly was born January 17th, 1825. He died, January 23d, 1841, aged 19 years and 5 days.

(5) Martin B. Nissly was born September 1st, 1829.

The following three children of (3) Bishop Samuel Nissly were by his second wife, Anna Mumma, widow of —— Greider.

(4) Jacob Nissly was born December 16th, 1800. He died, January 23d, 1875, aged 74 years, 1 month and 7 days. He married, in 1822, Barbara Wittwer, daughter of Preacher Daniel an d Anna Wittwer,

of East Earl township, Lancaster Co., Pa. Her brothers and sisters are, Isaac, married to Franey Sensenig ; Anna, married to Jacob Sensenig ; Catharine, married to John Horst ; Dr. Daniel, died single ; Benjamin, married to Catharine Snader and Barbara Ludwig ; David, married to Catharine Erb; Michael, married to Margarette Yundt ; Elisabeth, married to Abraham Buckwalter.

(4) Jacob and Barbara (Wittwer) Nissly begat children, viz:

(5) Anna Nissly was born November 3d, 1822. She married Joseph Summy, son of John and Elisabeth Summy. Their children are,

(6) Fannie Summy, married to Benjamin Minnich. They live in Maryland. Their children are, (7) Hiram, (7) Anna, (7) Joseph, (7) Daniel, (7) Lizzie, (7) Emma, (7) Benjamin.

(6) Abraham Summy, married to Mary Ann Stehman. Their children are, (7) Amanda, (7) John. Abraham Summy married the second time, Fannie (Hoffer) Ruhl (widow). She had one child with her first husband, name, Susan Ruhl. Their children are, (7) Anna, (7) Jacob, (7) Abraham.

(6) Barbara Summy, married to Isaac Zimmerman. Their children are, (7) Joseph, (7) Isaac, (7) Anna, (7) Elam.

(6) Mary Summy, married to Amos Moyer. Their children are, (7) John, (7) Joseph, (7) Emma.

(6) Jacob Summy, married to Kate Shreiner. Their children are, (7) Ada, (7) Lillie, (7) Lottie.

(6) Anna Summy.

(6) Lizzie Summy, married to Peter Will. Their children are, (7) Elmer, (7) Joseph Summy.

(5) Daniel Nissly was born August 28th, 1824. He went to Ohio. There he married Ellen Renfrew. Their children are,

(6) Jacob Nissly, (6) Rufus Nissly, (6) Ellen Nissly, (6) Harriet Nissly.

(5) Harriet Nissly was born March 29th, 1827.

(5) Jacob Nissly was born July 6th, 1830. He married Susan Mentzer, daughter of Jacob and —— Mentzer. Their children are, (6) Jacob Nissly, (6) Henry Nissly, (6) Samuel Nissly, (6) Anna Nissly, (6) John Nissly, (6) Barbara Nissly, (6) Amos Nissly, (6) Harvey Nissly, (6) Daniel Nissly.

(5) Barbara Nissly was born August 19th, 1832. She married Benjamin Metzler, son of John and Esther Metzler. Their children are,

(6) Daniel Metzler ; (6) Susan Metzler,

married to Jacob Hottenstein ; (6) Harriet Metzler; (6) Jacob Metzler; (6) Barbara Metzler; (6) Anna Metzler.

(5) Jemimi Nissly was born November 29th, 1834. She died in 1834.

(4) Henry Nissly was born in 1805. He died in March, 1841. He married Maria Nissly, daughter of Martin and Elisabeth Nissly, of Londonderry township, Dauphin Co., Pa. Her brothers and sisters are, Nancy Nissly, married to John Hagy, of Dauphin Co.; Elisabeth Nissly, married to Preacher Jacob Mumma, of Cumberland Co., Pa.; Barbara Nissly, married to Martin Nissly, of Derry township, Dauphin Co.; Jacob Nissly, married to —— Hursh; Fanny Nissly, married to Jacob Reif; Catharine Nissly, married to John Risser, of Lebanon Co., Pa.

(4) Henry and Maria (Nissly) Nissly begat children, viz:

(5) David N. Nissly, born May 3d, 1826, died November 14th, 1852, aged 26 years, 6 months and 11 days. He was married to a daughter of John Hammaker, near Elizabethtown, Lancaster Co., Pa.

(5) Elisabeth Anna N. Nissly, born December 11th, 1827, died September 18th, 1831, aged 3 years, 9 months and 7 days.

(5) Simon N. Nissly, born March 14th,

1830, died June 16th, 1831, aged 1 year, 3 months and 2 days.

(5) Annie N. Nissly, born April 16th, 1832, died January 26th, 1840, aged 7 years, 9 months and 10 days.

(5) Fannie N. Nissly, born November 25th, 1834, She married November 8th, 1855, Henry Shelly. Their children are,

(6) Samuel N. Shelly, married to Ella Coover. Their children are, (7) Carrie, (7) Nissly, (7) Annie.

(6) Elias N. Shelly; (6) David N. Shelly; (6) Lizzie N. Shelly; (6) Annie Shelly.

(5) Andrew N. Nissly, born November 1st, 1837, died January 9th, 1841, aged 3 years, 2 months and 8 days.

(4) Veronica Nissly was born June 21st, 1798. She died October 30th, 1839, aged 41 years, 4 months and 9 days. She married Abraham Huber, son of Abraham and —— Huber. They had one daughter, viz: Anna Huber, married to John Bassler. Their children are, Jacob; Amos; Fannie, married to Benjamin Landis. Anna (Huber) Bassler married the second time, Daniel Kreider. Their children are, Daniel; Mary; Esther; John.

Abraham Huber died. His widow married the second time, December 12th, 1819, Jonas Eby, son of John and Maria (Wittwer) Eby, of Elisabeth township, Lancaster Co., Pa. This family is described in the "Eby" family.

WE NOW RETURN TO (4) MARTIN NISSLY.

(4) Martin Nissly was born November 6th, 1788. He married, in 1810, Anna Bomberger, daughter of Joseph and Magdalena Bomberger, of Warwick township, Lancaster Co., Pa. Joseph Bomberger was a son of Christian Bomberger, which was a son of Christian and Maria Bomberger, who, with their two sons and six daughters emigrated from Eshlebrun in unterm Kœnigreich, gross Herzogthum, Baden, Germany, to America, in the year 1722. They settled in Lancaster county near where Lititz now is. Her mother was a daughter of Christian and Anna Hershey. Christian Hershey was born in 1719, and died in 1782. His wife Anna, was born in 1737; died in 1812. Her grandmother, Anna Hershey, was a daughter of Christian Hernly. This Anna Hernly was born on the Atlantic Ocean, 3 weeks before her parents landed in America.

Anna Bomberger, wife of (4) Martin Nissly, was born February 28th, 1791; died December 2d, 1881, aged 90 years, 9 months and 4 days. It is remarkable that both Martin Nissly and his wife Anna, were of the fourth generation of their respective families in America.

The following is a description of Anna Bomberger's brothers and sisters,

(4) Christian Bomberger (Bishop), was born September 18th, 1786. He died February 4th, 1871, aged 84 years, 4 months and 14 days. He married, December 9th, 1806, Barbara Erb, (born February 19th, 1790, died August 17th, 1834, aged 44 years, 5 months and 29 days), daughter of Daniel and Elizabeth (Bomberger) Erb. Her brothers and sisters are,

Catharine Erb, married to Samuel Hoffer. Their children are, Daniel, Eliza, George, Samuel, John, Jacob, Christian, Isaac.

Elisabeth Erb, married to John Miller. Their children are, Daniel, Henry, John, Reuben, Joseph, Susan, Lizzie, Catharine.

Daniel Erb, married to Mary Wittwer. Their children are, Daniel, John, David, Elisabeth, Maria, Anna, Catharine.

Joseph Erb, married to Nancy Stehman. They had one son—Daniel.

John Erb (Preacher), married to Fannie Bergy, their children are, Samuel, John (Preacher), Fannie, Elisabeth, Susan, Mary, Nancy, Barbara, Catharine, Martha.

Jacob Erb, married to Mary Bucher. Their children are, Jonas, Daniel, Jacob, Eliza, Susan, Anna, Catharine.

(4) Christian and Barbara (Erb) Bomberger begat children, viz:

(5) Elisabeth Bomberger, born October 23d, 1809, died August 27th, 1881, aged 71 years, 10 months and 4 days.

(5) Joseph Bomberger, born October 13th, 1811, died March, 1823, in the eleventh year of his age.

(5) Christian Bomberger, born October 16th, 1813. He married, in 1835, Mary Brubacher, (born July 6th, 1817), daughter of Joseph and Mary (Bucher) Brubacher. Her brothers and sisters are, Catharine, married to John Bomberger; Joseph, married to Susan Rudy; Barbara, married to Christian B. Snyder; David (Deacon), married to Eliza Hess; Eliza, married to Levi Weaver; Levi B., married to Eliza Sheaffer; Jonas, married to Leah Keller; John, married to Eliza Weidler; Anna, married to Jacob Sherk.

(5) Christian and Mary (Brubacher) Bomberger begat children, viz:

(6) Reuben B. Bomberger, born December 13th, 1836, married to Margarette Mateer. Their children are, (7) Clara, (7) Mary, (7) Minnie, (7) Christian, (7) Abbie.

(6) Barbara B. Bomberger, born December 4th, 1840, married to David M. Fogelsanger. Their children are, (7) Will D., (7) Edward B., (7) Anna Mary, (7) Christian, (7) Harry, (7) Frank, (7) David, (7) Lydia Belle, (7) Joseph, (7) Samuel, (7) Hulbert, (7) Elisabeth, (7) Reuben, (7) Thomas.

(6) Eliza B. Bomberger and Mary B. Bomberger, twins, were born June 30th, 1844, Eliza died September, 1861; Mary died May, 1845.

(5) Daniel Bomberger, born August 25th, 1815. He died October 9th, 1854. He married Martha Hull, November 20th, 1838. Their children are,

(6) Mary Bomberger, married to Samuel B. Fox. They live in Canton, Ohio. Their children are, (7) George, (7) Bertie, (7) Lilly, (7) Maud, (7) Abner, (7) Magdalena, (7) Jennie, (7) Adam, (7) Ula, (7) Bessie.

(6) Elisabeth Bomberger, married to Urias B. Schlott. They live in Fayette Co., Illinois. Their children are, (7) Lena Rivers, (7) Dio Louis, (7) Daniel Edward, (7) Viola.

(6) Adam W. Bomberger. married to Susan J. Archer. They live in Cleveland, Ohio.

They have one daughter, (7) Annie Magdalena Bomberger.

(6) Martha Magdalena Bomberger, single.

(6) Cyrus Bomberger, married to Helen Margarette Messner. Their children are, (7) Daniel E. Bomberger, (7) Nellie Bomberger, (7) Adam C. Bomberger.

(5) Isaac Bomberger, born August 22d, 1819. He married, October 19th, 1841, Sarah Wenger. They had no children.

(5) Fannie Bomberger, born October 26th, 1821.

(5) John Bomberger, born December 12th, 1823, died July 2d, 1846, aged 22 years, 6 months and 21 days.

(5) Joseph Bomberger, born April 16th, 1825, died October 27th, 1879, aged 54 years, 6 months and 11 days. He married, August 6th, 1846. Maria Kauffman. Their children are,

(6) Addison Bomberger, married to Fannie Weaver. Their children are, (7) Tobias, (7) Kate. (7) Frank.

(6) Lucinda Bomberger.

(6) Edwin Bomberger.

(6) Annie Bomberger, married to Jacob Zook. Their children are, (7) Elsie, (7) David, (7) Jacob.

(6) Christian Bomberger, married to

Anna Yost. Their children are, (7) Mervin, (7) Nebenger, (7) Nellie.

(6) Kate Bomberger, married to Joseph Blair. Their children are, (7) Bertie.

(6) Lizzie Bomberger, (6) Jacob Bomberger, (6) Levi Bomberger, (6) Amelia Bomberger.

(5) Magdalena Bomberger, born October 3d, 1817. She married, November 22d, 1836, George Baer. Their children are,

(6) Ephraim Baer, married to Hettie Hartman. Their children are, (7) George, (7) John, (7) Annie, (7) Lizzie, (7) May, (7) Emma.

(6) Christian Baer, married to Christiana Naze. Their children are, (7) Kate, (7) John.

(6) Isaac Baer.
(6) George Baer.
(6) Mary Baer, married to George White. Their children are, (7) Nathan, (7) Mary.

(6) Caroline Baer, married to Benjamin Donaphin. They have one child, (7) Cora.

(5) Barbara Bomberger, born June 13th, 1827.

(5) Anna Bomberger, born May 22d, 1833. She married Martin Berkheimer. Their children are,

(6) Samuel Berkheimer, married to Susan

Forry. Their children are, (7) Jennie Edith.
(6) Henry Berkheimer; (6) Annie Berkheimer; (6) Lizzie Berkheimer; (6) George Berkheimer.

(4) Elisabeth Bomberger was born October·7th, 1793. She died March 11th, 1871, aged 77 years, 5 months and 4 days. She married in 1815, Jacob Gingrich, son of David and Elisabeth Gingrich. His brothers and sisters are. David, married to Elisabeth Eby; Joseph, married to Sarah Gantz; Daniel, married to Catharine Hoffer; Henry, married to Polly Stover; Abraham, single; Christian, single. Jacob Gingrich was born September 14th, 1786. He died May 4th, 1872, aged 85 years, 7 months and 21 days.

(4) Jacob and Elisabeth (Bomberger) Gingrich begat children, viz :

(5) Benjamin Gingrich, born April 4th, 1818.

(5) A son was born January 14th, 1820, lived only 2 days.

(5) Eliza Gingrich, born February 18th, 1824. She married Elias Eidneier, son of Jacob and Maria Eidneier. His brothers and sisters are, Jacob, married to Rosanna Mummeldollar; John, married to Nellie Buchter; Henry, married to Mary Stauffer;

Abraham, married to Eliza Kraft; Elisabeth, married to Jessie Buchter; Maria, married to Henry Stauffer; Catharine, married to William Hornberger; Leah, married to Edward Wagner.

(5) Elias and Eliza (Gingrich) Eidneier begat children, viz:

(6) Maria Eidneier.

(6) Harriet Eidneier, married to Isaac Nasinger. Their children are, (7) Maria, (7) Amanda, (7) Amelia.

(6) Jacob Eidneier. married to Mary Helter. Their children are, (7) Stella, (7) Ezra. (6) Jacob Eidneier married, the second time, Peggy Meck. Their children are, (7) Nathan, (7) Jacob, (7) Lizzie, (7) Amanda, (7) Anna.

(6) Eliza Eidneier, married to Adam Showers. Their children are, (7) Amanda, (7) Harvey. (7) Elias, (7) Jacob, (7) Lizzie, (7) Anna, (7) Adam, (7) Emma, (7) Monroe.

(6) Lydia Ann Eidneier, married to Allen Hacker. Their children are, (7) Horace, (7) Samuel, (7) Harry, (7) Ada, (7) Wilson, (7) Adaline, (7) William.

(6) Amanda Eidneier, married to John Fassnacht. Their children are, (7) Henry, (7) Lizzie, (7) William, (7) Amanda.

(6) Anna Eidneier, married to George

Druckenbrod. Their children are, (7) Sallie, (7) Franklin.

(5) Anna Gingrich, born October 17th, 1826, died November 26th, 1842, aged 16 years, 1 month and 9 days.

(5) Sarah Gingrich, born Nov. 6th, 1828.

(5) Martin Gingrich and (5) Magdalena Gingrich were born August 13th, 1831. Martin died March 7th, 1852, aged 20 years, 6 months and 25 days. Magdalena married David Stroble. Their children are, (6) Henry, (6) Sallie. Magdalena died August 17th, 1865, aged 34 years and 4 days.

(5) Ephraim Gingrich was born May 30th, 1834. He lived only 3 months.

(4) Magdalena Bomberger was born January 27th, 1799. She married Preacher Christian Nissly. This family is described in the "Nissly" family.

(4) Maria Bomberger was born in 1800, died in 1851. She married Christian Weaver, (born in 1798, died in 1846), son of Joseph and —— (Burkholder) Weaver. His brothers and sisters are, Joseph Weaver; David Weaver; Nancy Weaver, married to —— Stauffer; Susan Weaver, married to —— Wenger; Mary Weaver, married to —— Frick; Martha Weaver.

(4) Christian and Maria (Bomberger)

Weaver lived in Ohio. They begat children, viz:

(5) Martha Weaver, married to Benjamin Hernly. Their children are. (6) Malinda, Hernly, married to Calvin M'Cord; (6) Edwin Hernly, married to Lilly Kingsby; (6) Benjamin Hernly, married to Mollie Davis; (6) Miles Hernly; (6) Franklin Hernly; (6) Lavina Hernly.

(5) John Weaver, married to Mary Charles. Their children are, (6) Emanuel Weaver; (6) John Weaver; (6) Hattie Weaver.

(5) Joseph Weaver, married to —— Shumbock. Their children are, (6) Setarah Weaver; (6) John Weaver.

(5) Mary Weaver, married to Hugh Gladwish. Their children are, (6) John Gladwish; (6) Martha Gladwish; (6) Helen Gladwish; (6) Frances Gladwish; (6) Stephen Gladwish.

(4) Joseph Bomberger (Preacher), was born July 12th, 1801. He died February 9th, 1869, aged 67 years, 6 months and 25 days. He married, February 2d, 1826, Sarah Erb, daughter of Jacob and Elisabeth (Becker) Erb. She was born April 28th, 1805. Her father, Jacob Erb, was born March 7th, 1781, died July 10th, 1864. Her mother, Elisabeth (Becker) Erb, was born

May 14th, 1782, died July 1st, 1812. Her brothers and sisters are,

Anna Erb, married to Christian Kauffman. Their children are, ten sons and three daughters.

Elisabeth Erb, married to Elias Eby, mentioned in the "Eby" family.

Catharine Erb, married to David Witmer. Their children are, Jacob, Franklin, and ten daughters.

Mary Erb, married to Elias Bomberger; they lived in West Virginia; their children are, Lizzie, married to Thomas Ault; Samuel, married to —— ——.

Henry Erb, married to Elisabeth Spickler; their children are, Reuben, married to Anna Grosh; Isabella, married to Jacob Mayer.

Levi Erb, married to Mary Wissler; their children are, Mary Ann, married to Frank Wissler; Lizzie, married to Dr. R. W. Stone.

(4) Joseph and Sarah (Erb) Bomberger begat children, viz:

(5) Jacob E. Bomberger, born January 27th, 1827. Married, December 31st, 1850, to Catharine Landis, (born July 3d, 1828), daughter of David and Catharine (Landis) Landis. Her brothers and sisters are, Christian, married to Catharine Musser;

Fannie, married to John Weltmer; Susan, married to Henry Myers; Sarah, married to John Smith; Mary, married to Zacharias Newcomer; David, married to Julia Brownewell and Catharine Smith; Henry, married to Caroline ——.

(5) Jacob E. and Catharine (Landis) Bomberger begat children, viz:

(6) Harry C. Bomberger, born May 14th, 1853, married to Susan Cressler, daughter of John H. and Elisabeth Cressler. Their children are, (7) Loudon L., (7) Mary E., (7) Florence.

(6) Anna Mary Bomberger, born October 11th, 1855, married to B. Franklin Koser, son of David and Margarette Koser.

(6) Sallie C. Bomberger, born January 26th, 1858, married to David R. Frehm, son of Jacob and —— Frehm. Their children are, (7) Jacob Erb Frehm.

(6) Stephen Jacob Bomberger, born February 11th, 1862, died November 11th, 1874, aged 12 years and 9 months.

(6) Minnie E. Bomberger, born October 16th, 1865.

(5) Magdalena Bomberger, born December 29th, 1828. She died July 3d, 1873, aged 44 years, 6 months and 5 days. She married, in 1849, Henry Cockley (born De-

cember 31st, 1827), son of Samuel and Susan Cockley.

(5) Henry and Magdalena (Bomberger) Cockley begat children, viz:

(6) Noah B. Cockley, born May 7th, 1850. He married, in 1877, Mary Ann Widders, daughter of Joseph and Elisabeth Widders. Their children are, (7) Sarah Elisabeth, born May 9th, 1879, died September 10th, 1879; (7) Emma Eve, born November 28th, 1880, died March 29th, 1882.

(6) Sarah Cockley, born January 8th, 1852. She married, in 1878, William Brindle, son of Solomon and Sarah Brindle.

(6) Susan Cockley, born May 25th, 1854.

(6) John Cockley, born May 14th, 1858, died October 8th, 1878.

(6) Joseph Cockly, born November 26th, 1859. He married in 1881, Emma C. Shaeffer, daughter of Henry and Peggy Shaeffer.

(6) Harry Cockley, born Jan. 2d, 1863.

(6) Magdalena Cockley, born Aug. 31st, 1864.

(6) Benjamin Cockley, born February 4th, 1867, died November 27th, 1872.

(6) Samuel Cockley, born November 8th, 1869, died December 26th, 1872.

(6) Anna Cockley, born April 14th, 1873, died August 23d, 1873.

(5) Henry Cockley, the father married the second time in 1876, Sarah Mellinger; she was born October 3d, 1823.

(5) Elisabeth Bomberger was born April 4th, 1831. She died June 27th, 1871, aged 40 years, 2 months and 23 days. She married, in 1863, John Hayes, son of John and Anna Hayes. His brothers and sisters are,

Maria Hayes, married to Isaac Stickler; their children are, William, Sarah.

Samuel Hayes, married to Mary Ann Brown; their children are, John, William, Anna.

William Hayes, died young; Martha Hayes, died young; Nancy Hayes.

(5) John and Elisabeth (Bomberger) Hayes begat children, viz:

(6) Anna B. Hayes, born March 4th, 1864.

(6) Sarah B. Hayes, born May 16th, 1865.

(6) John B. Hayes, born November 25th, 1867.

(6) Joseph B. Hayes, born July 18th, 1870.

(5) Anna Bomberger was born May 7th, 1832. She married, in 1850, George Gochenauer, son of Michael and Nancy Gochenauer. Their children are,

(6) Joseph Gochenauer, married (in 1879) to Amanda Leas, daughter of Valentine

Leas. Their children are, (7) Anna Louisa.

(6) Michael Gochenauer married (in 1875) to Ellen Kapp, daughter of Henry Kapp. Their children are, (7) Alice, (7) Lizzie, (7) Cora, (7) Henry.

(6) Simon Gochenauer, married (in 1880) to Kate Ellaker.

(6) Christian Hoover Gochenauer.

(5) Sarah Bomberger was born January 20th, 1834. She married, December 29th, 1853, Noah Cockley, son of Samuel and Susan Cockley. His brothers and sisters are, Samuel, Benjamin, David, John, Jacob, Henry, Joseph, Catharine, Mattie, Leah, Mary, Susan.

(5) Noah and Sarah (Bomberger) Cockley begat children, viz :

(6) Mattie Cockley, born October 22d, 1854. She married, October 29th, 1877, Abraham Lehman, son of Samuel and Catharine Lehman. Their children are, (7) Sarah C. Lehman, born September 24th, 1878; (7) Annie Lehman, born December 21st, 1881.

(6) Reuben Cockley, born January 13th, 1857. He married, December 2d, 1879, Annie Weaver, daughter of Preacher Henry and Susan Weaver. Their children are, (7) Noah W. Cockley, born October 18th,

1880; (7) Henry W. Cockley, born January 24th, 1882.
(6) Samuel Cockley, born November 27th, 1859.
(6) Henry Cockley, born April 9th, 1867.
(6) Sarah Cockley, born December 27th, 1869.

(5) Maria Bomberger was born June 23d, 1836. She married, in 1865, Isaac Eberly, son of Joseph and Susan (Hess) Eberly, of Clay township, Lancaster Co., Pa. Their children are,
(6) Rebecca Eberly, born February 2d, 1868; Sarah Eberly, born October 1st, 1870. These two were born in Cumberland Co.; Jacob Eberly, born May 2d, 1874; Reuben Eberly, born August 11th, 1876; Benjamin Eberly, born September 8th, 1878. These three were born in Franklin Co., Pa.

(5) Catharine Bomberger was born September 2d, 1838. She married, in 1866, Daniel Lehman (died January 22d, 1883), son of Peter and Susan Lehman. Their children are, (6) Joseph, (6) Anna, (6) Henry.

(5) Barbara Bomberger was born November 1st, 1840. She married, in 1860, John D. Lehman, son of Peter and Susan Lehman. Their children are, (6) Willie, died

September 2d, 1862; (6) Sadie ; (6) Lizzie; (6) David; (6) Susie.

(5) Rebecca Bomberger was born November 17th, 1842. She married, in 1868, Isaac Hurst, son of Joseph and Anna Hurst. Their children are, (6) Sadie ; (6) Stephen, died March 4th, 1881.

(5) Fannie Bomberger, born May 14th, 1844.

(5) Joseph Bomberger, born August 22d, 1847. He married, in 1873, Mattie Frantz, daughter of Isaac and Anna Frantz.

(5) Susie Bomberger was born August 13th. 1850.

(4) John Bomberger was born September 26th, 1803. He died December 24th, 1868, aged 65 years, 2 months and 28 days. He married November 20th, 1826, Catharine Brubacher, (born November 20th, 1808, died March 19th, 1837, aged 28 years, 3 months and 29 days), daughter of Joseph and Maria (Bucher) Brubacher. Her brothers and sisters are mentioned in the "Bomberger" family in Cumberland Co.

(4) John and Catharine (Brubacher) Bomberger begat children, viz :

(5) Elias B. Bomberger, born November 23d, 1827. He married, in 1856, Eliza Hammaker, daughter of Daniel and Fannie (Forry) Hammaker, of East Hempfield

township, Lancaster Co., Pa. Her brothers and sisters are mentioned in the "Hammaker" family. Eliza Hammaker was born February 28th, 1832, died April 13th, 1864, aged 32 years, 1 month and 15 days.

(5) Elias B. and Eliza (Hammaker) Bomberger begat children, viz :

(6) Elias Bomberger, married to Minnie Erisman. Their children are, (7) Bessie.

(6) Fannie Bomberger; (6) Lincoln Bomberger; (6) John Bomberger; (6) Lizzie Bomberger; (6) Mary Bomberger.

(5) Elias B. Bomberger married the second time, in 1875, Maria Hammaker, daughter of Daniel and Fannie (Forry) Hammaker.

(5) Joseph B. Bomberger, was born December 21st, 1828. He married in 1850, Fannie Risser, daughter of Preacher John and Elisabeth (Hess) Risser, of Elisabeth township, Lancaster Co., Pa. Her brothers and sisters are,

Preacher Jacob Risser, married to Fannie Eby. Mentioned in the "Eby" family, of Maryland.

John Risser, married to Eliza Ann Brackbill. Their family is mentioned in the "Nissly" family.

Lizzie Risser, married to Daniel Leed. Their children are, Harry.

Catharine Risser, married to John Buch. Their children are, Harvey, Lizzie, Aaron.

Martha Risser, married to Reuben Reist. Their children are, Anna, Mary, Sarah, Fannie, Martha, Lizzie, Katie.

Mary Risser, married to Joseph Oberholtzer. Their children are, Mary, Anna, Joseph.

Samuel Risser, single.

Fannie Risser was born August 16th, 1831, died November 8th, 1877, aged 46 years, 3 months and 22 days.

(5) Joseph B. and Fannie (Risser) Bomberger begat children, viz:

(6) Henry R. Bomberger, married to Lizzie Earhart. Their children are, (7) Anna, (7) Theda, (7) Elmer Scott, (7) Harry Hayes, (7) Abraham Garfield, (7) Minnie.

(6) Anna R. Bomberger, married to Samuel Ehrhart. Their children are, (7) Annie, (7) Fannie.

(6) Fannie R. Bomberger; (6) John R. Bomberger; (6) Joseph R. Bomberger; (6) Amos R. Bomberger.

(5) Mary B. Bomberger was born March 19th, 1830. She married, in 1853, George Hoffer, son of Emanuel and Barbara (Thuma) Hoffer. His brothers and sisters are,

Anna Hoffer, married to Henry Becker. Their children are, Eliza.

Samuel Hoffer, married to Anna Froelich. Their children are, Frank, Emma, Hiram, Samuel.

Elisabeth Hoffer, married to Peter Hammer. Their children are, Hiram, Emma, Emanuel, Lizzie, Harvey.

Christian Hoffer, married to Mary Gibble. Their children are, Barbara, Mary, Emanuel, Lizzie.

Catharine Hoffer, married to David Smith. Their children are, Samuel, Barbara.

(5) George and Mary B. (Bomberger) Hoffer begat children, viz:

(6) Fannie Hoffer, married to Henry Ruhl. They had one child, Susan.

(6) Fannie (Hoffer) Ruhl was married the second time, to Abraham Summy, mention in the "Nissly" family.

(6) Allen Hoffer, married to Fannie Hershey, daughter of Benjamin and Mary (Brubacher) Hershey. Their children are, (7) Mary.

(6) Henry Hoffer; (6) Emanuel Hoffer; (6) Catharine Hoffer.

(5) David B. Bomberger was born December 28th, 1831. He married Susan Weidman, daughter of David and Elisabeth Weidman, of Penn township, Lancaster Co., Pa. Her brothers and sisters are mentioned in the "Snyder" family.

(5) David B. and Susan (Weidman) Bomberger begat children, viz:
(6) Lizzie Bomberger; (6) Lavina Bomberger; (6) Catharine Bomberger; (6) Panini Bomberger; (6) Anna Bomberger.

(5) John B. Bomberger was born March 10th, 1833. He married Grace Robinson, daughter of William and —— Robinson. Her brothers and sisters are, Susan Robinson, married to Dr. George Ross; Ann Robinson, married to Joseph Detweiler.

(5) John B. and Grace (Robinson) Bomberger begat children, viz:
(6) William Bomberger; (6) Jennie Bomberger; (6) Martin Bomberger; (6) Mary Grace Bomberger.

(5) Magdalena B. Bomberger, born November 24th, 1834, died Sept. 27th, 1835.

(5) Catharine B. Bomberger. born July 22d, 1836, died September 1st, 1836.

The mother of the above family—Catharine (Brubacher) Bomberger—died in 1837.

(4) John Bomberger married the second time in 1837, Rebecca Eby, daughter of John and Maria (Wittwer) Eby, of Warwick township. Lancaster Co., Pa. Her brothers and sisters are described in the "Eby" family. Rebecca Eby was born December 3d, 1803, died November 21st, 1852, aged 48 years, 11 months and 18 days.

(4) John and Rebecca (Eby) Bomberger begat children, viz:

(5) Martin E. Bomberger, born December 12th, 1839. He married Martha Eisenberger.

(5) Sem E. Bomberger, born April 28th, 1842, died March 14th, 1872, aged 30 years and 17 days.

(5) Christian E. Bomberger, born February 2d, 1845. He married Catharine Miller. Her sister Anna was married to Henry Bealor. Their children are, Catharine, Lizzie. The mother, Rebecca (Eby) Bomberger, died in 1852.

(4) John Bomberger married, the third time, Elisabeth Shelly, widow of Jacob Shelly, and daughter of John and Anna (Snavely) Eberly, of Cumberland Co. Her brothers and sisters are, Jacob Eberly, married to Mary Zent; John Eberly, married to Elizabeth Nissly; Samuel Eberly, married to Susan Gerber and Fannie Gerber; Catharine Eberly, married to Jacob Rupp and Preacher Jacob Mumma.

(4) Barbara Bomberger was born in 1805. She died June 24th, 1872, in the 67th year of her age. She married Jacob Wissler, son of Jacob and Anna (Eby) Wissler, of Clay township, Lancaster Co., Pa. His brothers

and sisters are mentioned in the "Eby" family.

(4) Jacob and Barbara (Bomberger) Wissler begat children, viz:

(5) Anna B. Wissler, married to Christian Hess, son of Christian and Barbara Hess. His brothers and sisters are, John, Samuel, Abraham, Joseph, Catharine, Anna, Fannie, Barbara, Magdalena, Elisabeth.

(5) Christian and Anna B. Hess begat children, viz:

(6) Jacob W. Hess, married to Laura Reist. Their children are, (7) Clara, (7) Anna.

(6) Emanuel W. Hess; (6) John W. Hess; (6) Mary W. Hess; (6) Levi W. Hess; (6) Anna W. Hess.

(5) Jacob B. Wissler, married to Anna Brubacher, daughter of Joseph and Susan (Rudy) Brubacher. She had one sister, Lavina, married to Abraham L. Lane.

(5) Jacob B. and Anna (Brubacher) Wissler begat children, viz:

(6) Joseph B. Wissler, married to Lizzie Buch. Their children are, (7) Minnie, (7) Jacob.

(6) Lizzie B. Wissler, married to Christian B. Risser.

(6) Samuel B. Wissler; (6) Christian B. Wissler; (6) Susan B. Wissler.

(5) Martha B. Wissler, married to Samuel R. Hess, son of John and —— Hess. His brothers and sisters are, Mary, Jacob R., Elisabeth, Martha, Esther, Anna, John R. (Preacher).

(5) Samuel R. and Martha B. (Wissler) Hess begat children, viz :

(6) Anna E. Hess, married to Benjamin D. Heller. Their children are, (7) Samuel H., (7) Harvey H., (7) Benjamin H., (7) Jacob H., (7) John H.

(6) Israel W. Hess, married to Anna Doster. Their children are, (7) Alvin D., (7) Joseph Walter, (7) Martha.

(6) Susan W. Hess.

(6) Samuel A. Hess, married to Mary Longenecker. Their children are, (7) Abraham L.

(6) Mary W. Hess ; (6) Jacob W. Hess ; (6) Elias W. Hess ; (6) Lizzie W. Hess ; (6) Emma W. Hess ; (6) Sarah W. Hess ; (6) Barbie W. Hess ; (6) Menno W. Hess.

(5) Mary B. Wissler, married to Peter B. Rohrer, son of Jacob and Mary Rohrer, of East Hempfield township, Lancaster Co., Pa. His brothers and sisters are, Henry, Jacob, Elisabeth, Kate, Magdalena, Maria.

(5) Peter B. and Mary B. (Wissler) Rohrer begat children, viz :

(6) Anna W. Rohrer, married to Abra-

ham L. Lehman. Their children are, (7) Mary R.
(6) Barbie Ella Rohrer; (6) Jacob W. Rohrer; (6) Mary Kate Rohrer; (6) Peter Bachman Rohrer.
(5) Levi B. Wissler, died young.
Here ends the "Bomberger" family.

RETURN AGAIN TO (4) MARTIN AND ANNA (BOMBERGER) NISSLY.

The following is a description of their family:
(5) Magdalena Nissly, born June 25th, 1814. She married, in 1834, Sem Brubacher, son of Jacob and Maria (Eby) Brubacher.
The following is a description of the sisters of (5) Magdalena Nissly, daughter of (4) Martin and Anna (Bomberger) Nissly.
(5) Barbara Nissly was born February 11th, 1818. She died, May 13th, 1868, aged 50 years, 3 months and 2 days. She married, in 1837, Joseph W. Nissly, son of Preacher Martin and Anna (Wittmer) Nissly, of East Donegal township, Lancaster Co., Pa. Preacher Martin Nissly's brothers and sisters are,
Preacher Christian Nissly, married to

Maria Kraybill. Their children are, John Nissly (Deacon), Peter Nissly (Preacher), and Jacob Nissly.

Anna Nissly, married to Jacob Stauffer. This family is mentioned in the "Stauffer" family.

Preacher Martin Nissly's wife, Maria, was a daughter of Joseph and Barbara Wittmer, of Mount Joy township, Lancaster Co., Pa. Her brothers and sisters are, Peter Wittmer, married to —— ——; Samuel Wittmer, married to Fannie Brubacher; Christian Wittmer, married to Elisabeth Kolb ; Maria Wittmer, married to Henry Snyder ; Barbara Wittmer, married to Daniel Wohlgemuth; Catharine Wittmer, married to Jacob Hershey (Preacher) ; Frany Wittmer, married to John Horst.

Joseph W. Nissly, born July 21st, 1813. His brothers and sisters are,

Anna Nissly, married to Joseph Ebersole. Their children are, Noah, Anna, Martin, Joseph.

Barbara Nissly, married to Daniel Heisey.

Fannie Nissly, married to Jacob Snyder. Their children are, Joseph, Aaron, Peter, Mary, Anna.

Martin W. Nissly, married to Mary S.

Nissly. Their children are, Eli, Anna, Barbara, Fannie.

Mary Nissly, married to Philip Greiner. Their children are, Malinda, Fannie.

(5) Joseph W. and Barbara (Nissly) Nissly, begat children, viz:

(6) Ephraim N. Nissly (Preacher), born March 21st, 1841. He married, November 8th, 1864, Fannie N. Eby, daughter of Levi and Anna (Nissly) Eby, of Rapho township, Lancaster Co., Pa. Her sisters are described in the "Eby" family. Fannie N. Eby was born December 21st, 1843, died June 12th, 1871, aged 27 years, 5 months and 21 days.

(6) Preacher Ephraim N. and Fannie N. (Eby) Nissly begat children, viz:

(7) Barbara Nissly, born September 7th, 1865, died September 19th, 1870, aged 5 years and 12 days.

(7) Ellen Nissly, born August 13th, 1867, died January 17th, 1870, aged 2 years, 5 months and 4 days.

(7) Martha Nissly, born August 19th, 1870, died July 8th, 1871, aged 10 months and 19 days.

(6) Preacher Ephraim N. Nissly married the second time, January 9th, 1873, Mary Meckley (born August 1st, 1851), daughter

of Samuel and Fannie (Horst) Meckley. Her brothers and sisters are,

Henry Meckley, married to Amanda Nissly, daughter of Christian H. and Barbara Nissly. Their children are, Katie, Ada, Samuel, Fannie, Ellen.

Anna Meckley, married to Christian Flory, son of Christian and Lizzie (Sherk) Flory. Their children are, Anna, Henry.

Fannie Meckley, married to Joseph Masterson, son of Joseph and Anna Masterson. Their children are, Cora, Meckley, Irwin, Fannie, Simon.

Catharine Meckley, married to John Lindemuth, son of Martin and Anna Lindemuth.. Their children are, Emily, Katie.

(6) Preacher Ephraim N. and Mary (Meckley) Nissly begat children, viz :

(7) Anna Nissly, born Oct. 15th, 1873.

(7) Frances Nissly, born September 19th, 1875, died October 6th, 1880, aged 5 years and 18 days.

(7) Emma Nissly, born Dec. 4th, 1877.

(7) Joseph Nissly, born Feb. 5th, 1881.

(7) Samuel Nissly born April 10th, 1883.

(6) Martin N. Nissly was born June 4th, 1843, died March 14th, 1844, aged 9 months and 10 days.

(6) Elias N. Nissly was born February 15th, 1845. He married, October 31st,

1869, Rebecca N. Eby, born October 4th, 1850, daughter of Levi and Anna (Nissly) Eby, of Rapho township, Lancaster Co., Pa. Her sisters are mentioned in the "Eby" family.

(6) Elias N. and Rebecca N. (Eby) Nissly begat children, viz :
(7) Gabriel Nissly, born Nov. 28th, 1870.
(7) Fannie Nissly, born Oct. 23d, 1873.
(6) Anna N. Nissly was born May 5th, 1849. She married, November 1st, 1870, Harry S. Kraybill (born June 6th, 1849), son of Peter and Fannie (Snyder) Kraybill, of West Donegal township, Lancaster Co., Pa. His brothers and sisters are,

Levi S. Kraybill, married to Anna G. Longenecker. Their children are, Emma, Lizzie, Mary.

Christian S. Kraybill, married to Susan Engle.

Peter S. Kraybill, married to Sarah Lehman.

Samuel S. Kraybill, married to Mary G. Reist. mentioned in the " Reist" family.

Tillman ; Frances S. Kraybill ; Mary S. Kraybill.

(6) Harry S. and Anna N. (Nissly) Kraybill begat children, viz:
(7) Matilda N. Kraybill, born July 3d, 1872.

(7) Phares N. Kraybill, born June 24th, 1875.
(7) Bertha N. Kraybill, born June 7th, 1879.

RETURN AGAIN TO (5) ANNA NISSLY.

(5) Anna Nissly was born August 22d, 1819; she died April 11th, 1845, aged 25 years, 7 months and 20 days. She married, September 22d, 1840, Emanuel Cassel, son of Abraham and Magdalena (Ehrisman) Cassel, of Rapho township, Lancaster Co., Pa. Abraham Cassel was a son of Abraham Cassel. Emanuel Cassel's brothers and sisters are,

Dr. John H. Cassel, married to —— ——. Their children are,

Charles G. Cassel.

Clara M. Cassel, married to Thomas Morris.

Mary Cassel, died single.

Jacob E. Cassel, married to Mary Winebrenner; their children are, Ellen, William, Harriet, Jane, Harry, Laura, Emma, Charles, Sadie.

Hettie Ann Cassel, married to John K. Barr; their children are, Mary, Frank, Martha, Abraham, Anna.

(5) Emanuel and Anna (Nissly) Cassel begat children, viz :
(6) Abraham N. Cassel, born August 25th, 1843. He married Anna Longenecker.
(6) Anna N. Cassel, born March 26th, 1845 ; she married October 1st, 1863, Henry B. Hertzler, son of John B. and Elisabeth (Brenneman) Hertzler. His brothers and sisters are mentioned in the "Brubacher" family.
(6) Henry B. and Anna N. (Cassel) Hertzler begat children, viz :
(7) Anna Elisabeth Hertzler, born May 5th, 1864.
(7) Henry Milton Hertzler, born June 12th, 1865.
(7) Fannie C. Hertzler, born August 2d, 1866.
(7) Emanuel Cassel Hertzler, born December 12th, 1869.
(7) John C. Hertzler, born Feb. 10th, 1874.
(7) Elam C. Hertzler, born May 26th, 1876.
(7) Nora Grace Hertzler, born October 21st, 1878.
(5) Emanuel Cassel married the second time Maria Rohrer, daughter of John and Susan Rohrer, of Rapho township, Lancaster Co., Pa. Her brothers and sisters are,

Jacob Rohrer, married to Susan Baker; their children are, Amelia, Benjamin, Barbara, Anna, Susan.

John K. Rohrer, married to Catharine and Mary Hiestand, daughters of Christian Hiestand. Their children are, Allan, Martha, Susan, John, Clinton, Christian, David, Frank, Harvey, Malinda, Phares, Paris, Mabel.

Christian K. Rohrer, married to Mary Greider. Their children are, Emma, Minnie, Ellen, Harry, Emerson, Mary, Christian.

Anna K. Rohrer, married to Andrew D. Hershey.

David K. Rohrer, died young.

(5) Emanuel and Maria (Rohrer) Cassel begat children, viz:

(6) Mary Cassel; (6) Susan Cassel, married to Aaron Kling; their children are, (7) Grace, (7) Bessie.

(6) Lizzie Cassel, married to Amos M. Greider. Their children are, (7) Harry, (7) Benjamin Franklin, (7) Charles, (7) Howard, (7) Christian.

(6) Emanuel R. Cassel; (6) Hettie R. Cassel; (6) John R. Cassel; (6) Emma R. Cassel, married to John Eby; (6) Clara R. Cassel; (6) Harry R. Cassel.

Return again to (5) Fannie Nissly.

(5) Fannie Nissly was born December 3d, 1821. She married, in 18—, Jacob W. Snyder, son of Henry and Maria (Wittmer) Snyder, of West Donegal township, Lancaster Co., Pa. His brothers and sisters are,

Barbara Snyder, married to Deacon John Nissly. Their family is mentioned in the "Eby" family.

Mary Snyder, married to Joseph B. Nissly. Their children are, Samuel Nissly, married to Magdalena Kreider; John Nissly; Catharine Nissly, married to Christian H. Stauffer; Joseph S. Nissly, married to Maria Stauffer: Mary Nissly, married to Abraham F. Root; Lizzie Nissly.

Catharine Snyder.

Anna Snyder, married to Christian Hoffman. Their children are, Eli Hoffman, married to Fannie Lindemuth; Fannie Hoffman, married to Abraham Engel; Christian Hoffman, married to Elisabeth Gerber; Anna Hoffman, married to John Forny; Lizzie Hoffman; Martha Hoffman, married to John Shenk.

Christian W. Snyder, married to Mary Gerber and Fannie H. Stauffer. Their children are, John G. Snyder, married to

Fianna N. Eby, mentioned in the "Eby" family; Henry G. Snyder, married to Anna Bomberger; Christian G. Snyder, married to Susan Flory; Anna G. Snyder, married to Christian N. Newcomer; Jacob S. Snyder; Mary S. Snyder, married to Amos W. Newcomer; Reuben S. Snyder; Fannie W. Snyder, married to Peter Kraybill. This family is mentioned in the "Nissly" family.

(5) Jacob W. and Fannie (Nissly) Snyder begat children, viz:

(6) Jacob N. Snyder, born in 1849. He married in 1868, Harriet S. Weidman, daughter of David and Elisabeth (Stehman) Weidman, of Penn township, Lancaster Co., Pa. Her brothers and sisters are,

Lizzie S. Weidman, married to Joseph Buckwalter. Their children are, Hiram, Lizzie, Anna, Henry, David, Daniel, Joseph.

Barbara S. Weidman, married to Jacob N. Newcomer. Their children are mentioned in the "Nissly" family.

John S. Weidman, married to Fannie Cassel. Their children are, Lizzie, Barbara, John, Frances.

Susan S. Weidman, married to David B. Bomberger, mentioned in the "Bomberger" family.

Henry S. Weidman, mentioned in the "Snyder" family.

Anna S. Weidman, married to Tobias Hershey. Their children are, Lillie.

(6) Jacob N. and Harriet S. (Weidman) Snyder begat children, viz :

(7) Phares W. Snyder, born June 26th, 1869.

(7) Jacob W. Snyder, born December 18th, 1877.

(6) Fannie N. Snyder was born March 12th, 1852. She married, in 1870, Henry S. Weidman, (born March 10th, 1848), son of David and Elisabeth (Stehman) Weidman, of Penn township, Lancaster Co. His brothers and sisters have been mentioned above.

(6) Henry S. and Fannie N. (Snyder) Weidman begat children, viz :

(7) Fannie S. Weidman, born September 24th, 1871.

(7) Harry S. Weidman, born October 3d, 1873.

(7) Amanda S. Weidman, born December 31st, 1875.

(7) Ellen S. Weidman, born July 14th, 1878.

(7) Jacob S. Weidman, born June 11th, 1881.

(6) Mary Ann N. Snyder, born July 8th,

1855. She married, in 18—, John B. Harnish, son of Deacon Jacob and Martha (Brubacher) Harnish, of East Hempfield township, Lancaster Co., Pa. His brothers and sisters are, Susan B. Harnish, married to Henry H. Stauffer; Henry B. Harnish; Jacob B. Harnish.

(6) John B. and Mary Ann N. (Snyder) Harnish begat children, viz:

(7) Fannie S. Harnish, born September, 1875; (7) John S. Harnish, born October, 1880.

(6) Barbara N. Snyder, born November 5th, 1859.

(6) Henry N. Snyder, born November 14th, 1862.

RETURN AGAIN TO (5) MARIA NISSLY.

(5) Maria Nissly was born June 17th, 1824. She married, in 1846, Benjamin Musser (born February 14th, 1825), son of Benjamin and Barbara (Miller) Musser, of East Hempfield township, Lancaster Co., Pa. His brothers and sisters are,

Abraham Musser, died single.

Martha Musser, married to John Shenk. Their children are, Henry, Benjamin, Susan.

Anna Musser, married to Jacob Herr.

Their children are, Amanda, Benjamin, Hebron, Jacob, Frank, Amos, Mary Ann.

Barbara Musser, died young.

Elisabeth Musser, married to Benjamin Baer. Their children are, Barbara, Susan, Lizzie, Benjamin, Henry.

John Musser, married Catharine Nissly. Their children are, Anna, Lizzie, Benjamin, John, Fannie, Amos.

(5) Benjamin and Maria (Nissly) Musser begat children, viz:

(6) Martin N. Musser, born December 25th, 1847. He married, in 1869, Anna Seitz, daughter of John and Mary (Mellinger) Seitz, of East Hempfield township, Lancaster Co., Pa. Her brothers and sisters are,

Susan, married to Abraham Herr. Their children are, Anna, Abraham, Ella.

Mary, married to Henry Stehman; Emma; Jacob.

(6) Martin N. and Anna (Seitz) Musser begat children, viz:

(7) Mary S. Musser, born August 2d, 1872; (7) Henry S. Musser, born May 24th, 1874.

(6) Anna N. Musser was born September 21st, 1849. She married, in 1871, Joseph H. Cassel, son of John and Mary (Hernly)

Cassel, of Penn township, Lancaster Co., Pa. His brothers and sisters are,

Anna H. Cassel, married to Jacob S. Hershey. Their children are, Louisa, Lizzie.

Maria H. Cassel.

Henry H. Cassel, married to Anna Minnich. Their children are, Milton, Amanda, Nora, Anna.

Lizzie H. Cassel.

John H. Cassel, married to Adaline W. Kreider. Their children are, Fannie, Anna, John.

(6) Joseph and Anna N. (Musser) Cassel begat children, viz :

(7) Amos M. Cassel, born December 19th, 1872; (7) Emma M. Cassel, born August 24th, 1874; (7) Frank M. Cassel, born July 21st, 1882.

(6) Barbara N. Musser was born July 11th, 1852. She married, in 1872, Abraham Cassel, son of Jacob and Barbara (Hernly) Cassel, of Rapho township, Lancaster Co., Pa. His sisters are,

Fannie H. Cassel, married to John S. Weidman (mentioned elsewhere).

Anna H. Cassel, married to John N. Musser. Their children are, Minnie.

(6) Abraham and Barbara N. (Musser) Cassel begat children, viz :

(7) Henry M. Cassel was born August 15th, 1873.

(6) Benjamin N. Musser was born February 1st, 1854, died September 29th, 1860, aged 6 years, 7 months and 28 days.

(6) Mary N. Musser was born June 22d, 1858.

(6) Henry N. Musser was born September 8th, 1868, died March 2d, 1869, aged 5 months and 22 days.

END OF DESCRIPTION OF (5) MAGDALENA (NISSLY) BRUBACHER'S SISTERS. NOW RETURN TO

(5) Sem and Magdalena (Nissly) Brubacher begat two sons, viz:

(6) Martin N. Brubacher, born October 11th, 1835, in Elisabeth township, Lancaster Co. The parents moved to Rapho township, Lancaster Co., Pa, in 1836. He married, October 26th, 1856, Mary Ann Snavely (born September 28th, 1837), daughter of Henry and Mary Ann (Stauffer) Snavely, of Penn township, Lancaster Co. Her brother, Henry S. Snavely, married Barbara B. Reist, described in the "Reist" family.

Henry Snavely was a son of Jacob and

Elisabeth Snavely, of Rapho township, Lancaster Co. His brothers and sisters are,

Jacob Snavely, died single.

Isaac Snavely, married to Mary Gingrich; they lived in Lebanon Co., Pa. Their children are,

Jacob, married to Anna Hershey. Their children are, Mary, Elisabeth, Henry, Andrew, Jacob, Emma, Anna, Samuel, Isaac.

Christian, single.

John, married to Elisabeth Hagy. Their children are ——.

Elisabeth, married to John Bachman. Their children are, William, Lizzie, Joseph.

Mary, married to Hiram Sechrist. Their children are, Lizzie, John, Frederick, Henry.

Anna; Martha; Martin; Joseph; Fannie; Isaac.

John Snavely was born 1795. He married, in 1821, Anna Hershey, daughter of Preacher Benjamin and Veronica (Snyder) Hershey, of Penn township, Lancaster Co. Her brothers and sisters are mentioned in the "Brubacher" family. John and Anna (Hershey) Snavely begat children, viz:

Fannie Snavely, married to John Stehman. Their children are, Jacob, John, Mary.

Elisabeth Snavely.

Abraham Snavely, married to Anna Brubacher. Their children are, Henry, Daniel, Fannie, Benjamin, Anna, Phares, Susan, Abraham, Mary, Lizzie.

Jacob H. Snavely (Preacher), married to Susan Brubacher. Their children are, Mary Ann, John, Jacob, Phares, Amos, Susan.

John Snavely.

Benjamin H. Snavely, married to Eliza Brubacher. Their children are, John, Lizzie, Benjamin, Samuel, Phares, Emma, Eli.

Jonas H. Snavely, married to Lizzie Hertzler. Their children are, Sarah, Fannie, Anna, Jacob, John, Jonas.

David H. Snavely, married to Anna S. Gingrich, mentioned in the "Gingrich" family.

Anna H. Snavely, married to Owen Heiser. Their children are, John.

Samuel H. Snavely, married to Anna Hernly. Their children are, Amanda, Emma, Peter, Samuel, Anna, Henry.

Henry Snavely was born September 26th, 1801. He married, in 1832, Mary Ann Stauffer (born January 28th, 1811), daughter of Martin and Maria (Kauffman) Stauffer. Her parents are described in the "Stauffer" family.

(6) Martin N. and Mary Ann (Snavely) Brubacher begat one daughter, viz: (7) Fannie S. Brubacher.

(6) Jacob N. Brubacher (Bishop) was born July 25th, 1838. He married, November 1st, 1857, Barbara H. Stauffer (born July 15th, 1833), daughter of David K. and Anna (Hammaker) Stauffer, of Rapho township, Lancaster Co.

(6) Jacob N. and Barbara H. (Stauffer) Brubacher begat children, viz:

(7) Enos S. Brubacher, born and died March 14th, 1859.

(7) Fannie S. Brubacher, born July 25th, 1860, she died January 10th, 1865, aged 4 years, 5 months and 15 days.

(7) Martin S. Brubacher, born July 23d, 1862. He married, December 11th, 1883, Emma Frances Wittmer, daughter of Christian and Magdalena (Hoffman) Wittmer, of Silver Springs, Lancaster Co.. Emma Frances Wittmer was born June 26th, 1860. Her brother and sister are,

Salina H. Wittmer, born July 17th, 1863.
Clayton H. Wittmer, born Jan. 6th, 1867.

Christian Wittmer was a son of John and Maria (Hoffman) Wittmer, of Rapho township, Lancaster Co. His brothers and sisters are,

Mary, married to David Becker. Their

children are, Elmira, Emma, Phares, David.

Barbara, married to Henry Becker. Their children are, Anna, Mary.

Lizzie, married to Henry M. Stauffer. Their children are, Emma, Mary, Harry.

Fannie, single.

Samuel, married to Catharine Becker. Their children are, Phema, Alice, Samuel, John.

Henry, married to —— ——.

Amos, married to Kate Brenneman. Their children are, John, Mary, Amos, Morris, Katie.

Dr. Eli, married to Ellen Sutton.

Christian Wittmer's wife was a daughter of John and Catharine (Balmer) Hoffman, of East Hempfield township, Lancaster Co. Her sisters are,

Anna, married to Henry Baer and Christian Mumma. Their children are, John Baer, Susan Baer, and Simon Mumma.

Adaline, married to Abraham Stauffer. Their children are, Mary Ann, Emma, Katie, Hiram, Milton.

Susan, married to Reuben Longenecker. Their children are, Torrence, Anna.

(7) David S. Brubacher, born May 5th, 1867, died January 12th, 1870, aged 2 years, 8 months and 7 days.

(7) Magdalena S. Brubacher, born December 11th, 1869.

(7) Sem S. Brubacher, born September 29th, 1872.

THE FOLLOWING IS A DESCRIPTION OF DAVID K. AND ANNA (HAMMAKER) STAUFFER'S ANCESTORS AND BROTHERS AND SISTERS.

David K. Stauffer, was a son of Martin and Maria (Kauffman) Stauffer.

Martin Stauffer was a son of John and Barbara (Amweg) Stauffer.

John Stauffer was a son of Christian Stauffer.

Christian Stauffer had two sons, John and Jacob. Whether he had more children cannot be ascertained. He was born in Germany, on the "Mueckenhæuserhof," in Wartenberg, in the Pfalz. He had three brothers; the name of one was John, who was born August 6th, 1715, in Germany. He married Catharine Shenk, of Conestoga, Lancaster Co.

(1) Christian Stauffer, his two sons, three brothers, and his mother emigrated to America, though in what year cannot be as-

certained. These four sons hauled their mother, by hand, on a little wagon, from their home in Germany, to the ship. After they landed in Philadelphia, they procured a wagon again, and hauled their mother from Philadelphia through the wilderness to the Hammer Creek, about 4 miles north of Lititz, Lancaster Co., where they settled and founded a "mill seat," known for many years as "Stauffer's mill." On their journey from Philadelphia, one of the sons was lost. No doubt he lost himself in the wilderness. It was a noble work of those four sons to haul their mother, and stands as a monument of that filial affection which all children owe to their parents.

(2) John Stauffer was born March 26th, 1734. He died January 13th, 1799, aged 64 years, 9 months and 17 days. He married Barbara Amweg (born November 11th, 1738, died October 15th, 1809, aged 70 years, 11 months and 4 days), daughter of John Martin and Barbara (Wissler) Amweg. They settled in "Gruben land." Thence they moved to a mill seat on the Big Chiquis creek, about two miles east of Mount Hope, which they bought of a man by the name of Lentz.

(2) John and Barbara (Amweg) Stauffer begat children, viz: John, Jacob, Joseph,

Christian, Martin, Anna, Barbara, Catharine, Maria; of these the following grew up and were married.

(3) John Stauffer, married to —— Kolb. Of this family no trace can be found.

(3) Jacob Stauffer was born October 22d, 1770. He died April 14th, 1802, aged 31 years, 5 months and 22 days. His death was caused by falling from a horse. He married Anna Nissly (born January 16th, 1774, died November 6th, 1856, aged 82 years, 9 months and 20 days), daughter of Martin and Anna Nissly, of Mount Joy township, Lancaster Co. Her brothers and sisters are, Preacher Christian Nissly, married to Maria Kraybill; Preacher Martin Nissly, married to Anna Wittmer.

(3) Jacob and Anna (Nissly) Stauffer begat children, viz:

(4) John Stauffer was born December 31st, 1796. He married Elisabeth Miller, she was born November 13th. 1799, died February 26th, 1844, aged 44 years, 3 months and 13 days. Their children are, (5) Benjamin M., (5) Anna, (5) Jacob M., (5) Tobias M., (5) Aaron, (5) Elias M.

(4) Anna Stauffer, married to Christian Hershey. Their children are, (5) Esther, (5) Jacob, (5) Maria, (5) Anna, (5) Christian.

(4) Catharine Stauffer, married to John Huber. Their children are, (5) John S., (5) Anna, (5) Eli, (5) Henry.

(4) Jacob Stauffer, married to Catharine Hershey, mentioned in the "Hershey" family.

(3) Joseph Stauffer was born February 23d, 1773. He died December 9th, 1853, aged 79 years, 11 months and 16 days. He married to Catharine Acker (born August 27th, 1780, died June 10th, 1855, aged 74 years, 9 months and 13 days), daughter of Henry and Maria Acker, of Rapho township, Lancaster Co.

Henry Acker was born March 7th, 1745, died March 14th, 1825, aged 80 years and 7 days.

Maria Acker was born in 1758, died in 1824, in her 66th year.

(3) Joseph and Catharine (Acker) Stauffer begat children, viz:

(4) Jacob Stauffer, born November 1st, 1804, died August 17th, 1806.

(4) Henry Stauffer, born April 13th, 1802. He married, March 12th, 1822, Anna Cassel, daughter of Joseph and —— Cassel. Her brothers and sisters are, Joseph, died single; Henry, died single; David, married to —— Gibble; John, married to Anna Hernly and Anna Weaver; Jacob, married

to Barbara Hernly; Elisabeth, married to Henry Buckwalter; Mary, married to Jacob Hostetter.

(4) Henry and Anna (Cassel) Stauffer begat one son, viz:

(5) David Stauffer, died young.

Anna (Cassel) Stauffer, the mother, was born March 15th, 1804, died May 19th, 1824, aged 20 years and 22 days.

(4) Henry Stauffer married, the second time, Catharine Snyder (born August 27th, 1808, died July 27th, 1835, aged 26 years and 11 months), daughter of John and Elisabeth Snyder. Her brothers and sisters are, Anna; Elisabeth; Jacob, married to Adaline Rohrer; John, married to ——— Shollaw; Samuel, married to Fannie E. Nissly.

(4) Henry and Catharine (Snyder) Stauffer begat children, viz:

(5) Joseph S. Stauffer, married to Martha Buckwalter. Their children are, (6) Lizzie, (6) Henry, (6) Benjamin, (6) Mary Ann, (6) Reuben, (6) Amanda.

(5) Lizzie S. Stauffer, died young.

(5) Samuel S. Stauffer, married to Eliza Metzler.

(5) Anna S. Stauffer, died young.

(5) Maria S. Stauffer, died April 24th, 1855, aged 21 years, 7 months and 28 days.

(5) Henry S. Stauffer, married to Eliza Hershey. Their children are, (6) John, (6) Anna, (6) Susan, (6) Mary. The mother died, February 28th, 1862, aged 32 years, 3 months and 1 day.

(5) Henry S. Stauffer, married the second time, Barbara (Rutt) Reist (widow of Christian B. Reist). Their children are, (6) Martha, (6) David, (6) Benjamin, (6) Mary, (6) Emma.

(4) Catharine (Snyder) Stauffer, died in 1835.

(4) Henry Stauffer married, the third time, to Susan Eby (born March 4th, 1805, died April 27th, 1882, aged 77 years, 1 month and 23 days) daughter of Christian and Veronica (Hershey) Eby. Her brothers and sisters are mentioned in the "Eby" family.

(4) Henry and Susan (Eby) Stauffer begat children, viz:

(5) Jacob E. Stauffer, married to Barbara Mohn. Their children are, (6) Stella, (6) Bara, (6) Henry Wayne.

(5) Benjamin E. Stauffer, died young.

(5) Catharine E. Stauffer, married to Jacob G. Nissly. Their children are, (6) Susan, (6) Simon, (6) John, (6) Barbara, (6) Catharine.

(5) Veronica E. Stauffer, died young.

(5) Christian E. Stauffer, married to Susan Mohn. Their children are, (6) Milton, (6) Katie, (6) Ellen, (6) Henry.

(5) Susan E. Stauffer, married to Joseph E. Brubacher. Their children are, (6) Amon, (6) Clayton, (6) Ellie, (6) Henry, (6) Susan.

(4) Mary Stauffer, married to John Hostetter, son of Bishop Jacob Hostetter. Their children are, (5) Eliza, married to Jacob L. Stehman; (5) Sarah, married to Daniel Grosh; (5) Henry, married to Mary Ann Stehman.

(4) Catharine Stauffer, married to Samuel L. Brubacher. Their children are, (5) Joseph, married to Maria Moore and Harriet Hostetter; (5) Maria, married to Christian L. Miller; (5) Samuel, married to Rose Shelly; (5) Catharine.

(4) Elisabeth Stauffer, married to Jacob Kauffman. Their children are, (5) Jacob, married to Mattie Haas; (5) Henry, single; (5) Leah, married to Christian Myer; (5) Adaline, married to Samuel M. Stape; (5) Reuben, married to Harriet Dunlap; (5) John, married to Jessie Landis; (5) Emma, died.

(3) Christian Stauffer was born ——— ———. He died July 29th, 1798, aged ———.

(3) Anna Stauffer.

(3) Barbara Stauffer, married to Christian Knull. Their children are, (4) Barbara Knull, married to Michael Nafziger; (4) John Knull, married to Mary Moyer; (4) Christian Knull, married to Frany Landis; Maria Knull, married to D. Light. The family of Christian and Barbara (Stauffer) Knull live in Lebanon Co., Pa.

(3) Maria Stauffer (born December 3d, 1768, died April 2d, 1845, aged 76 years, 3 months and 29 days) married to Henry Acker. Their children are, (4) Jacob, (4) Anna, (4) Barbara, (4) John. Henry Acker died. His widow married, the second time, Christian Hershey, near Manheim, Lancaster Co., Pa.

(3) Christian Stauffer was born August 12th, 1792, died March 23d, 1793, aged 7 months and 11 days.

(3) Martin Stauffer (mentioned on page 156) was born November 15th, 1778. He died December 22d, 1873, aged 95 years, 1 month and 7 days. He married, May 4th, 1802, Maria Kauffman, daughter of Michael and Veronica (Bergy) Kauffman, of East Hempfield township, Lancaster Co., Pa. She was born December 9th, 1781, died September 5th, 1837, aged 56 years, 9

months and 6 days. Her brothers and sisters are,

John Kauffman, married to ———— ————. Their children are, John, Christian, Barbara, Anna.

Anna Kauffman, married to Joseph Gochenauer. Their children are, John, Jacob, Joseph, Henry, Michael, Elisabeth, Anna, Veronica, Magdalena, Mary, Martin.

Veronica Kauffman, married to Henry Musselman.

Barbara Kauffman, married to David Rohrer. Their children are, Simon, Michael, Benjamin, David, Fannie, Anna, Elisabeth.

David Kauffman, died single.

Andrew Kauffman, died single.

(3) Martin and Maria (Kauffman) Stauffer begat children, viz:

(4) David K. Stauffer was born April 19th, 1804. He died March 27th, 1866, aged 61 years, 11 months and 8 days. He married, January 28th, 1825, Anna Hammaker, daughter of Daniel and Anna (Musser) Hammaker, of West Hempfield township, Lancaster Co., Pa. Anna Hammaker was born September 17th, 1807, died September 28th, 1867, aged 60 years and 11 days. The following is a description of her parents, and brothers and sisters:

Daniel Hammaker was born April 15th, 1781. He died August 28th, 1862, aged 81 years, 5 months and 13 days. His brothers and sisters are, John Hammaker, married to —— Brenneman; Abraham Hammaker, married to Elisabeth Hiestand; Christian Hammaker, married to Anna Landis; Joseph Hammaker, married to Elisabeth Hoffman, Mary Berntheisel, and Adaline Strickler; Elisabeth Hammaker, married to Joseph Evans. Daniel Hammaker was a son of (1) John and Maria Hammaker, of West Hempfield township, Lancaster Co., Pa.

(1) John Hammaker was born in 1740. He died October 22d, 1804, in his 64th year. His wife's maiden name was "Bollinger." She was born in 1743, and died October 4th, 1821, in her 79th year.

(2) Daniel Hammaker married April 15th, 1806, Anna Musser, daughter of Henry Musser, of West Hempfield township, Lancaster Co., Pa. Anna Musser was born October 2d, 1790, died July 28th, 1847, aged 56 years, 9 months and 26 days. Her sister's name is Barbara Musser, married to Abraham Stauffer, of West Hempfield township, Lancaster Co., Pa.

(2) Daniel and Anna (Musser) Hammaker begat children, viz:

(3) Anna Hammaker (will be described elsewhere).

(3) Daniel Hammaker was born January 10th, 1811. He died August 26th, 1876, aged 65 years, 7 months and 16 days. He married, April 28th, 1830, Frances Forry, daughter of John and Veronica Forry, of Manor township, Lancaster Co., Pa. She was born April 20th, 1811, died November 17th, 1877, aged 66 years, 6 months and 27 days. Her mother's maiden name was "Seitz." She died November 3d, 1878, aged 103 years, 11 months and 17 days. Her brothers and sisters are,

Daniel Forry, married to Catharine Kauffman. Their children are, John, married to Mary N. Newcomer; Fannie, married to Christian Charles; Elisabeth, married to Christian Shuman; Maria, married to Jacob Stauffer; Isaac; Catharine, married to —— Rohrer.

Elisabeth Forry, single.

John Forry, married to Anna Landis. Their children are, Fannie, married to Joseph Charles; Anna, married to —— Eshbach; Daniel, married to —— Swarr; Elisabeth, married to —— Groff; Susan, married to —— Sensenig.

Jacob Forry, married to Mary Copenheffer. Their children are, John; Jacob, married to Elisabeth Eshleman.

Anna Forry, married to Harry Heise. Their children are, ———.

Susan Forry, married to David Harnish. Their children are, Fannie, married to —— Harnish; Jacob (Deacon), married to Martha Brubacher; Elisabeth, married to Henry Rohrer; Mary, married to Amos Herr; Anna; Leah, married to Henry Brubacher; David, married to Martha ——; Sarah, married to —— Harnish; Daniel, married to —— Weidler.

(3) Daniel and Frances (Forry) Hammaker begat children, viz:

(4) Anna Hammaker, born February 20th. 1831. She married, in 1850, John Rohrer, son of Daniel and Mary Rohrer, of East Hempfield township, Lancaster Co., Pa. His brothers and sisters are,

Anna Rohrer, married to Abraham Miller. Their children are, Mary, married to Israel Weber; Lizzie, Henry, Anna, Daniel, Hettie, Tobias, Fannie, Abraham, Emma, John, Jacob, Susan, Amos, David, Isaac, Martin, Alice.

Jacob Rohrer, married to Mary Kreider. Their children are, Jacob, married to Amanda Stauffer; Mary, married to Martin S. Nissly; Daniel, John, Hettie.

Daniel Rohrer, married to Lizzie Fisher. They live in Missouri. Their children are, Mary, Hettie, Anna, ——.

Esther Rohrer, died single.

Abraham Rohrer, married to Lizzie Eby. Their children are, Mary, Amos, Lizzie, Anna, Daniel, Fannie, Noah, Ira.

Isaac Rohrer, married to Emma Nance. They live in Missouri. Their children are, Alice, Hettie, Isaac.

Mary Rohrer, married to Isaac Stoner. Their children are, Rohrer, Ellen, Lizzie, Amie, Daniel, Stella.

(4) John and Anna (Hammaker) Rohrer begat children, viz:

(5) Emma Rohrer, married to Samuel B. Nissly, mentioned in the "Nissly" family.

(5) Fannie Rohrer, married to Noah Getz. Their children are, (6) Forry, (6) Noah, (6) Mabel, (6) Anna.

(4) Eliza Hammaker was born February 28th, 1832, described in the "Bomberger" family.

(4) Fannie Hammaker was born October 11th, 1833. She married, in 1855, Menno G. Wenger, son of Michael and Elisabeth Wenger, of West Earl township, Lancaster Co., Pa. His brothers and sisters are,

Marks G. Wenger, married to Maria

Graybill. Their children are, Graybill, Milton, Oped, Ceylon, Eliza, Annie, Emma.

Gabriel G. Wenger, married to Martha Herr. Their children are, Martin.

Michael G. Wenger, married to Susan Diller. Their children are, Levan, Annie, Lizzie.

Joel Wenger, married to Anna Swarr. Their children are, Clayton, Lincoln, Lizzie, Sue, Alice.

Mattie Wenger, married to Levi Groff. Their children are, Levi jr., Wenger, Maria, Lizzie, Amanda, Susan, Frances.

Maria Wenger, married to Christian Mellinger. Their children are, Abram, John.

Susan Wenger, married to Benjamin Westhaeffer. Their children are, William, Lizzie. Mary.

Lizzie Wenger, married to Benjamin Moyer. Their children are, Lincoln, Alfred, Lillie, Alice.

Fannie Wenger, married to Benjamin Groff.

(4) Menno. G. and Fannie (Hammaker) Wenger begat children, viz:

(5) Daniel H. Wenger.
(5) Joel H. Wenger.
(5) Annie H. Wenger, married to Daniel Weaver. They have two children.

(5) Mary H. Wenger, married to John Wissler. They have one child.
(5) Menno H. Wenger.
(5) Fannie H. Wenger.
(4) Maria Hammaker was born April 1st, 1836, died December 6th, 1883, aged 47 years, 8 months and 5 days. (Mentioned in the "Bomberger" family.)
(4) John Hammaker, died young.
(4) Barbara Hammaker was born June 26th, 1839. She married, in 1862, Philip Brehm, son of Philip and Barbara Brehm. His brothers and sisters are, Cyrus, married to —— Matzal; Maria, married to —— Gerber.
(4) Philip and Barbara (Hammaker) Brehm, begat children, viz:
(5) Anna Brehm, married to Jeremiah Baumgardner; (5) Amie; (5) Maria; (5) Fannie; (5) Hammaker; (5) Lizzie; (5) Edwin; (5) Frances; (5) Barbara; (5) Lyman.
(4) Daniel Hammaker was born April 1st, 1842. He married, in 18—, Lizzie Brandt, daughter of Daniel and Mary Brandt.
(4) Daniel and Lizzie (Brandt) Hammaker begat children, viz: (5) Clara, (5) Anna.
(4) Amos Hammaker was born June 20th,

1845, died September 30th, 1865, aged 20 years, 3 months and 10 days.

(4) David Hammaker was born March 28th, 1847. He married, in 1878, Frances Leopold, daughter of Henry and Sarah Leopold. Her brothers and sisters are, Rebecca, married to David Landis; Amanda; Harrison; Phares, married to Emma Walter; Anna, Henry, Walter, Sadie.

(4) David and Frances (Leopold) Hammaker begat children, viz:
(5) David Lyman; (5) Daniel; (5) Menno.

(3) Mary Hammaker was born August 1st, 1813.

(3) Barbara Hammaker was born October 10th, 1816.

RETURN AGAIN TO THE DESCRIPTION OF THE FAMILY OF (4) DAVID K. AND ANNA (HAMMAKER) STAUFFER.

(5) Mary H. Stauffer was born December 1st, 1825. She married, in 1843, Samuel Aungst, son of John and Catharine (Bergy) Aungst, of Dauphin Co., Pa. Samuel Aungst was born August 28th, 1819. His brothers and sisters are,

Benjamin Aungst, born August 30th, 1815.

Elisabeth Aungst, born February 8th, 1817, married to William Umberger. Their children are, Anna, William, Clara.

Isaac Aungst, born September 24th, 1823, married to Mary Hatz. Their children are, Mary, Ellen, Samuel, Isaac Newton.

Mary Aungst, born May 13th, 1829, died single.

Elias Aungst, born October 2d, 1833, died single.

Amos Aungst, born February 22d, 1837, married to Martha Smith. Their children are, Franklin, Katie.

(5) Samuel and Mary H. (Stauffer) Aungst begat children, viz:

(6) Anna S. Aungst, born December 24th, 1843, died May 31st, 1844, aged 5 months and 7 days.

(6) David S. Aungst, born September 6th 1845, died April 10th, 1874, aged 28 years, 7 months and 4 days.

(6) Catharine S. Aungst, born September 13th, 1847, died June 7th, 1867, aged 19 years, 8 months and 24 days.

(6) Henry Martin S. Aungst, born February 15th, 1850. He married, in 1880, Emma Beamesderfer, daughter of John and Lizzie Beamesderfer, of East Hempfield township, Lancaster Co., Pa. Their chil-

dren are, (7) Elmer B. Aungst; (7) Clara B. Aungst.

(6) Samuel S. Aungst, born October 25th, 1851. He married, in 1875, Kate Hornberger, daughter of Jeremiah and Mary Hornberger, of West Cocalico township, Lancaster Co., Pa.

(6) Samuel S. and Kate (Hornberger) Aungst begat children, viz:

(7) Harry H. Aungst, born December 30th, 1875.

(7) Alice H. Aungst, born May 27th, 1877, died August 2d, 1880, aged 3 years, 2 months and 5 days.

(7) Minnie H. Aungst, born April 15th, 1879.

(6) Mary Ann S. Aungst, born February 16th, 1854.

(6) Elias S. Aungst, born July 15th, 1855. He married, in 1877, Mary J. Stauffer, daughter of Henry and Anna Stauffer, of Brecknock township, Lancaster Co., Pa.

(6) Elias S. and Mary J. (Stauffer) Aungst begat children, viz:

(7) Bertha, (7) David F., (7) Annie.

(6) Barbara Emma S. Aungst, born May 5th, 1858.

(6) Phares S. Aungst, born May 4th, 1860.

(6) Elisabeth S. Aungst, born February 20th, 1862.

(6) Amos S. Aungst, born October 4th, 1864.

(6) Susan S. Aungst, born November 16th, 1866.

(6) Fannie S. Aungst, born March 15th, 1869.

(5) Anna H. Stauffer, born September 19th, 1828, died May 27th, 1850, aged 21 years, 8 months and 8 days.

(5) Fannie H. Stauffer, born June 11th, 1830. She married, December 7th, 1848, Christian E. Gingrich, son of David and Elisabeth (Eby) Gingrich. His mother was a daughter of Christian and Veronica (Hershey) Eby. His brothers and sisters are described in the " Eby" family.

Christian E. Gingrich was born September 25th, 1825.

(5) Christian E. and Fannie C. (Stauffer) Gingrich begat children, viz :

(6) Levi S. Gingrich, born January 13th, 1850. He married Mary Becker, daughter of Christian and Susan (Zeller) Becker. Her brothers and sisters are, Ezra Becker, single; Ellen Becker, married to Scott Little. Their children are, Stella.

(6) Levi S. and Mary (Becker) Gingrich begat children, viz :

(7) Clara N. Gingrich, born August 20th, 1879.

(7) Christian G. Gingrich, born September 4th, 1881.

(7) Levi Martin Gingrich, born October 8th, 1883.

(6) Anna S. Gingrich was born November 25th, 1852. She married in 18—, David H. Snavely, son of John and Anna (Hershey) Snavely, of Rapho township, Lancaster Co. His brothers and sisters are mentioned in the "Snavely" family.

(6) David H. and Anna S. (Gingrich) Snavely begat children, viz:

(7) Jacob G. Snavely, born August 19th, 1871.

(7) Ella G. Snavely, born December 11th, 1878, died November 21st, 1881, aged 2 years, 11 months and 10 days.

(6) David S. Gingrich, born November 14th, 1854, died February 24th, 1874, aged 19 years, 3 months and 10 days.

(6) Lizzie S. Gingrich, born July 18th, 1856,

(6) Fannie S. Gingrich, born August 18th, 1858. She married, in 18—, Jacob S. Weidman, son of David and Elisabeth (Stehman) Weidman, of Penn township, Lancaster Co., Pa. His brothers and sisters are mentioned in the "Snyder" family.

(6) Jacob S. and Fannie S. (Gingrich) Weidman begat children, viz:

(7) Christian G. Weidman, born May 27th, 1879.

(7) Phares G. Weidman, born October 18th, 1880.

(6) Christian S. Gingrich, born May 13th, 1861.

(6) Jonas S. Gingrich, born November 16th, 1862.

(6) Barbara S. Gingrich, born May 25th, 1865.

(6) Henry S. Gingrich, born September 29th 1867. He died May 13th, 1876, aged 8 years, 7 months and 14 days.

(5) Barbara H. Stauffer, born July 15th, 1833. She married Jacob N. Brubacher. This family is described on page 154.

(5) Susan H. Stauffer, born April 11th, 1836. She married, October —, 1856, Benjamin E. Nissly, son of Samuel and Anna (Eby) Nissly, of Rapho township, Lancaster Co. His brothers and sisters are described in the "Nissly" family.

(5) Benjamin E. and Susan H. (Stauffer) Nissly begat children, viz:

(6) Anna S. Nissly, born July 4th, 1857. She married, October 21st, 1880, Amos H. Frank, (born October 26th, 1858), son of John and Anna (Hess) Frank, of Manheim township, Lancaster Co. His brothers and sisters are, Christian H. Frank, married to

Anna Neff; Henry H. Frank; John H. Frank.

(6) Amos S. Nissly, born October 13th, 1859, died January 8th, 1860, aged 2 months and 26 days.

(6) Martin S. Nissly, born July 19th, 1861. He married October 27th. 1881, Mary K. Rohrer (born March 19th, 1862), daughter of Jacob and Mary (Kreider) Rohrer, of Rapho township, Lancaster Co. Her brothers and sisters are, Jacob K. Rohrer, married to Amanda Stauffer; John K. Rohrer; Esther K. Rohrer.

(6) David S. Nissly, born March 4th, 1863. He married, October, 1883, Mary B. Risser (born July 8th, 1863), daughter of John and Eliza Ann (Brackbill) Risser, of Warwick township, Lancaster Co. Her brothers and sisters are,

Abner Risser, married to Susan Miller. Their children are, Ellen, John, Wayne.

Barbara Ann Risser, married to Aaron Hess. Their children are, Amanda, Milton, Elias, Ada, Mary.

Phares Risser; Amos Risser.

Levi Risser, married to Lizzie Erb. Their children are, Ephraim.

Elias Risser, married to Sarah Bomberger. Their children are, Elmer, Isaac.

Eliza Risser, married to Peter Brubacher. Their children are, Ellen, Ada.

(6) Benjamin S. Nissly, born March 11th, 1866.

(6) Fannie S. Nissly and (6) Susan S. Nissly, born March 8th, 1868.

(6) Mary S. Nissly, born August 12th, 1876.

(5) David H. Stauffer was born August 27th, 1841. He died September 9th, 1854, aged 13 years and 13 days.

End of description of the family of (4) David K. and Anna (Hammaker) Stauffer.

RETURN AGAIN TO THE FAMILY OF (3) MARTIN AND MARIA (KAUFFMAN) STAUFFER.

(4) John Stauffer was born June 17th, 1806. He died November 29th, 1878, aged 72 years, 5 months and 12 days. He married, May 18th, 1837, Elisabeth Hostetter, daughter of Jacob and Anna (Swarr) Hostetter, of Manor township, Lancaster Co., Pa. Elisabeth Hostetter was born June 27th, 1813, died September 10th, 1870, aged 57 years, 2 months and 13 days.

(4) John and Elisabeth (Hostetter) Stauffer begat children, viz :

(5) Maria Stauffer, born February 8th, 1838. She married, January 17th, 1858, Joseph S. Nissly, son of Joseph B. and Mary (Snyder) Nissly, of Donegal township, Lancaster Co. His brothers and sisters are mentioned in the "Snyder" family. Joseph S. Nissly, died November 26th, 1861, aged 27 years, 4 months and 18 days. His widow, Maria (Stauffer) Nissly, married the second time, November 20th, 1865, Samuel N. Eby, son of Jonas and Veronica Eby. of West Hempfield township, Lancaster Co. His brothers and sisters are mentioned in the "Eby" family.

(5) A son was born December 2d, 1839 ; lived only a short time.

(5) Fannie Stauffer was born December 2d, 1840, died October 17th, 1846, aged 5 years, 10 months and 15 days.

(5) Emanuel R. Stauffer was born February 9th, 1844, died January 17th, 1866, aged 21 years, 11 months and 8 days.

(5) Henry S. Stauffer was born August 25th, 1846. He married, October 21st, 1866, Catharine Becker (born January 23d, 1846), daughter of John and Anna (Hoover) Becker, near Marietta, Lancaster Co.

(5) Henry S. and Catharine (Becker) Stauffer begat children, viz :

(6) Paris B. Stauffer, born September 7th, 1867.

(6) Nora Stauffer, born July 14th, 1869, died April 3d, 1872, aged 2 years, 8 months and 29 days.

(6) Howard B. Stauffer, born February 13th, 1871.

(6) Norman B. Stauffer, born August 6th, 1873, died October 17th, 1876, aged 3 years, 2 months and 11 days.

(6) Arthur Stephens Stauffer, born April 9th, 1875, died December 4th, 1877, aged 2 years, 7 months and 26 days.

(6) Miriam Stauffer, born December 1st, 1876.

(6) Elisabeth Stauffer, born June 23d, 1879.

(6) Edith Stauffer, born March 7th, 1881.

The brothers and sisters of Catharine Becker, wife of Henry S. Stauffer are,

Nathaniel Becker, died; Norman Becker, died.

Isabella Becker, married to Edwin L. Reinhold. Their children are, Edwin, Anna, Ethie, John Jay, ——, ——.

Emma Becker; Fremont Becker.

A DESCRIPTION OF CATHARINE BECKER'S PARENTS.

John Becker, married to Anna Hoover, daughter of John M. and Catharine (Stauffer) Hoover. Her brothers and sisters are,

John Hoover, married to Fannie Stehman. Had one son Clayton C. J. S. Hoover. John Hoover married, the second time, Mary Beltzhoover. Their children are, Henry M., George B., Annie E. L., John A. B.

Eli Hoover, married to Josephine Ream. Their children are, Ida, Ella.

Henry S. Hoover, married to Celia Childs. Their children are, Elmer, Miriam, Katie.

John Becker was a son of Henry and Maria S. (Bucher) Becker. His brothers and sisters are,

Catharine Becker, married to John Keener. They had four children, Levina, Hettie, Fianna, Susan.

Sarah Becker, married to Abraham Hess. They had nine children, viz: Henry, married to —— Buckwalter; Nancy, married to —— Rudy; Barbara, married to —— Rudy; Christian, married to —— Kurtz; Abraham, married to —— Keller; Sarah, married to —— Royer; Fianna, married to —— Landis; Hettie, married to —— ——; Susan, married to —— Stoner.

Nancy Becker, married to Jacob Hess. They had two children, viz: Susan, married to Henry Frank; Anna, married to Nathaniel Erb.

Elias Becker, married to Anna Stauffer. They had one son, Frank, married to Catharine Kline.

Henry Becker, married to Anna Bomberger. They had two children, viz: Elmira, married to John Graybill; Staunton, died.

Levi Becker, married to Anna Bruckhart. They had four children, viz: Daniel, Sabilla, Jeremiah, Lizzie.

Israel Becker, married to Carrie Buckwalter. They had five children, viz: Henry, married to Mary Seibert; John; Leah; Catharine; David.

Elisabeth Becker, married to Henry S. Brubacher, mentioned in "Brubacher" family.

John Becker had one step-brother and five step sisters, viz:

Maria, married to John Eby. They had one son, Jacob.

Fianna, married to Daniel Habecker.

They had two children, viz: Isabella, Daniel.

Leah, married to Abraham Bollinger. They had three children, viz: Amanda, Lizzie, Anna.

Susan, married to Henry Buch, they had one daughter.

Amanda, married to Samuel Pfantz, they had five children.

Reuben, married to Amanda Sharp, they had three children.

Henry Becker, the father of the above family, was a son of Christian and Nancy (Brubacher) Becker. His brothers and sisters are, Christian Becker, married to —— Kissel; Susanna Becker. married to L. Johns; —— Becker, married to —— Erb; Barbara Becker, married to J. Forney; Mary Becker, married to A. Eichler; Miss Becker, married to —— Snyder.

Christian Becker, the father, was a son of Arnold Becker. Arnold Becker had three children—Christian Becker, Peter Becker, —— Becker, married to Dr. Samuel Fahnestock. Arnold Becker was a son of Arnold Becker, who, with five brothers, came from Switzerland, Europe.

Return again to the family of John Stauffer.

(5) John K. Stauffer was born October 25th, 1848. He married, March 6th, 1879, Magdalena Herr, daughter of Henry and Elisabeth (Brenneman) Herr, of East Hempfield township, Lancaster Co. Her brothers and sister are, Jacob B. Herr, married to Lizzie Herr; Henry B. Herr, married to Levina Graybill; Emily Herr; Benjamin Herr; Amos Herr.

(5) Elisabeth Stauffer was born November 1st, 1852. She died October 31st, 1854, aged 1 year, 11 months and 30 days.

End of the family of (4) John Stauffer.

(4) Martin K. Stauffer was born October 1st, 1808. He died December 3d, 1854, aged 46 years, 2 months and 2 days. He married, in 1831, Elisabeth Kauffman, daughter of Andrew and Adaline (Shenk) Kauffman, of East Hempfield township, Lancaster Co. Elisabeth Kauffman was born August 18th, 1811. Her brothers and sisters are, John Kauffman, died young;

Andrew Kauffman, died young; John Kauffman, married to Maria Fidler; Jacob Kauffman, married to Elisabeth Stauffer; Henry Kauffman, married to Martha Peifer; Leah Kauffman, married to Henry Summy; Anna Kauffman, died single.

(4) Martin K. and Elisabeth (Kauffman) Stauffer begat children, viz:

(5) Henry K. Stauffer, born August 11th, 1832, died February 26th, 1839, aged 6 years, 6 months and 15 days.

(5) Maria K. Stauffer, born December 31st, 1833. She died February 16th, 1862, aged 28 years, 1 month and 16 days. She married Daniel Saylor. They had one child, viz: Lizzie S. Saylor, died.

(5) Leah K. Stauffer, born November 24th, 1835. She married John Herr. Their children are, (6) Jonas, (6) Lizzie, (6) Maria, (6) John Adams, (6) Ada.

(5) Harriet K. Stauffer, born February 5th, 1837, died March 4th, 1839, aged 2 years and 30 days.

(5) Fannie K. Stauffer, born February 28th, 1839, died May 29th, 1841, aged 2 years, 3 months and 1 day.

(5) Adaline K. Stauffer, born January 29th, 1842. She died April 7th, 1875, aged 33 years, 2 months and 8 days. She married Christian H. Newcomer. They begat

one son, viz: Morris S. Newcomer married Lucy Wright.

(4) Mary Ann K. Stauffer, mentioned in the "Snavely" family.

(4) Veronica K. Stauffer, born June 18th, 1813. She died August 29th, 1815, aged 2 years, 2 months and 11 days.

(4) Samuel K. Stauffer, born April 24th, 1816. He died September 29th, 1858, aged 42 years, 5 months and 5 days. He married Mehela Van Cannan. They had one son, viz: (5) Jefferson Stauffer.

(4) Henry K. Stauffer, born July 8th, 1820. He died August 24th, 1821, aged 1 year, 1 month and 17 days.

END OF DESCRIPTION OF THE "STAUFFER"

FAMILY.

(5) Henry E. Brubacher was born February 1st, 1815. He married, November, 1837, Mary Hershey, daughter of Christian and Susan (Baer) Hershey, of Penn township, Lancaster Co. Christian Hershey was a son of Christian and Elisabeth (Snyder) Hershey, of Penn township, Lancaster Co. His brothers and sisters are mentioned in the "Eby" family.

Mary Hershey was born September 19th,

1820. The name of her brother is, David Hershey (Deacon). He was born January 8th, 1817. He married, October, 1845, Fannie Hostetter, daughter of Bishop Jacob and Elisabeth Hostetter, of Penn township, Lancaster Co. Her brothers and sisters are,

John Hostetter, married to Polly Stauffer. Their children are, Eliza, Sarah, Henry. John Hostetter, married the second time to Eliza Forry. Their children are, Emanuel, Benjamin, John, Ephraim, Maria.

Mary Hostetter, died single.

Anna Hostetter, married to Christian Wissler. Their children are, Elisabeth, Benjamin, Jacob, Mary Ann.

Jacob Hostetter, married to Mary Cassel. Their children are, Harriet, Joseph, Anna.

Susan Hostetter, married to John Shaeffer. Their children are, Josiah.

Barbara Hostetter, married to Joseph Hershey. Their children are, Benjamin, Ephraim, Esther, Anna, Joseph.

Martha Hostetter, married to John Stauffer. Their children are, Lizzie, David.

David Hostetter, married to Maria Peifer. Their children are, Jacob P., Lizzie, Abraham, Martha, Josiah, David, Nathan, Sarah, Emanuel Cephas, Benjamin.

Catharine Hostetter, married to Christian

Ehrisman. Their children are, Susan, Lizzie, Metz, Sarah, Albert, Mary, Minnie.

David and Fannie (Hostetter) Hershey begat children, viz:
. Benjamin Hershey.

Susan Elisabeth Hershey, married to Simon K. Nissly. Their children are, David, Lizzie, Jacob, Fannie.

Amos Hershey, married to Lavina Hostetter. Their children are, Fannie.

David Christian Hershey, married to Kate Keller.

RETURN TO (5) HENRY E. AND MARY (HERSHEY) BRUBACHER.

(5) Henry E. and Mary (Hershey) Brubacher, begat children, viz:

(6) Isaac H. Brubacher born October 17th, 1839, He married, in 1863, Maria L. Huber, daughter of Samuel and Fannie (Brubacher) Huber. Her brothers and sisters are,

Abraham Huber, married to Susan Oberholtzer. Their children are, Fannie, Martha, Susan, John, Anna.

John Huber, married to Anna Horst. Their children are, Lizzie.

Anna Huber, married to Henry Kurtz. Their children are, Alice, Amanda, Aaron.

Fannie Huber, married to Henry Loos. Their children are, Catharine, Daniel, Samuel, David, Henry.

(6) Isaac H. and Maria B. (Huber) Brubacher begat children, viz:

(7) Amanda H. Brubacher, born January 13th, 1867.

(7) Mary H. Brubacher, born May 26th, 1871.

(7) Aaron H. Brubacher, born October 30th, 1875.

(6) Maria H. Brubacher was born September 22d, 1841. She married, in 1873, Jacob M. Rutt, son of David and Magdalena Rutt, of Manor township, Lancaster Co. His brothers and sisters are described in the " Reist" and " Nissly" families.

(6) Jacob M. and Maria H. (Brubacher) Rutt begat children, viz:

(7) Amelia B. Rutt, born April 5th, 1876.

(7) Ella B. Rutt, born December 27th, 1877.

(7) Jacob B. Rutt, born December 5th, 1880.

(6) Susan H. Brubacher was born December 24th, 1843. She married, in 1874, Benjamin D. Hershey, son of Abraham and Su-

san (Doner) Hershey, of Rapho township, Lancaster Co., Pa.

Benjamin D. Hershey was born February 11th, 1847, died September 12th, 1880, aged 33 years, 6 months and 28 days. His brothers and sisters are,

Andrew Hershey, married to Anna Rohrer.

John D. Hershey, married to Anna Mellinger. Their children are, Abraham Christian, John, Phares, Abner, Emma, Susan, Sarah, Benjamin, Anna, Elam, Mary.

Fannie Hershey, married to Benjamin B. Brenneman. Their children are, Susan, Frances, Mary, Anna.

Elisabeth Hershey, died young.

Mary Hershey, married to Benjamin D. Rohrer, of Illinois. Their children are, Abner, Hiram, Benjamin, Emma, Abraham, Henry, Susan, Mary, John.

Susan Hershey, married to Andrew Greider. Their children are, Anna, John, Susan, Abraham, Benjamin, Andrew.

Abraham Hershey, died young.

Sarah Hershey, married to Joseph E. Lehman. Their children are, Florence, Arthur.

(6) Benjamin D. and Susan H. (Brubacher) Hershey begat children, viz :

(7) Mary S. Hershey, born November 27th, 1875.

(7) Alliene Hershey, born May 27th, 1877, died March 31st, 1878, aged 10 months and 4 days.

(7) Harry B. Hershey, born July 17th, 1879.

(6) Jacob H. Brubacher was born March 14th, 1846. He married, in 1875, Elisabeth Shenk, daughter of Michael and Sarah (Horst) Shenk, of Lebanon Co., Pa. Her brothers and sisters are mentioned in the "Horst" family.

(6) Jacob H. and Elisabeth Shenk Brubacher begat children, viz:

(7) David S. Brubacher, born February 3d, 1877, died August 31st, 1878, aged 1 year, 6 months and 28 days.

(7) Mary S. Brubacher, born July 10th, 1879.

(6) Catharine H. Brubacher was born September 4th, 1848. She married, in 1871, Jacob B. Hertzler, son of John B. and Elisabeth (Brenneman) Hertzler. His brothers and sisters are, John B. Hertzler, married to Barbara Brubacher. Their children are, Andrew, Benjamin, Lizzie. He married the second time to Rebecca Strickler. Their children are, Amos, Barbara, Anna, Ellen, Jacob, Samuel.

Lizzie B. Hertzler, married to Ulrich Hertzler.

Christian B. Hertzler, married to Catharine Grossman. Their children are, Emeline, Phares, Agnes, Mary, David, Nathanael.

Anna Hertzler, married to Daniel Burkholder. Their children are, Anna, Daniel, Mary, Lizzie, Elam.

Benjamin Hertzler, married to Susan Lehman.

Fannie Hertzler, married to Frank Miller. Their children are, Nora.

Eli Hertzler, married to Sarah Harnish. Their children are, Franklin, Annie.

Mary Hertzler, married to Christian Andrews.

(6) Jacob B. and Catharine H. (Brubacher) Hertzler begat children, viz:

(7) Mary B. Hertzler, born August 12th, 1871.

(7) Harry B. Hertzler, born July 1st, 1874.

(7) John B. Hertzler, born August 8th, 1876.

(7) Ada B. Hertzler, born January 23d, 1879.

(7) Clayton B. Hertzler, born December 24th, 1880.

(7) Lizzie B. Hertzler, born May 18th, 1883.

(6) Sem H. Brubacher was born April 3d, 1853. He married, in 1880, Mary Walter, daughter of Peter and Catharine Walter. Her brother's name is Henry Walter.

(6) Sem H. and Mary (Walter) Brubacher begat children, viz :

(7) Henry W. Brubacher, born June 6th, 1881.

(6) Henry H. Brubacher, born March 28th, 1855. He married, in 18—, Fannie Kreider, daughter of Jacob and Anna Kreider, of East Hempfield township, Lancaster Co. Her brothers and sisters are,

Christian Kreider, married to Maria (Erb) Landis, widow. Their children are, Katie, Jacob.

Adaline Kreider, married to John Cassel. Their children are, Fannie, Anna, John.

Mary Ann Kreider, married to Martin Peifer. Their children are, Christian, Fannie, Ida, Anna, Jacob.

(6) Henry H. and Fannie (Kreider) Brubacher begat children, viz :

(7) Anna K. Brubacher, born October 6th, 1877

(7) Elam K. Brubacher, born November 15th, 1879.

(7) Lizzie K. Brubacher, born September 25th, 1881.

(6) Ephraim H. Brubacher, born July

9th, 1859, died July 27th, 1860, aged 1 year and 18 days.

RETURN AGAIN TO (5) ISAAC BBUBACHER.

(5) Isaac Brubacher was born March 11th, 1817. He married, September 13th, 1841, Rebecca Hershey, daughter of Andrew and Mary (Hoffman) Hershey, of West Hempfield township, Lancaster Co.

Andrew Hershey was a son of Abraham and ——— (Kreider) Hershey. Rebecca Hershey was born March 23d, 1815, died August 25th, 1850, aged 35 years, 5 months and 2 days. Her brothers and sisters are,

Abraham Hershey, married to Susan Donor. Their family is mentioned in the "Brubacher" family.

Liza Hershey, died young.

Fannie Hershey, married to Abraham Kreider. They had one child, died young.

Mary Hershey, married to Christian Herr. They had one daughter, died young.

Jacob Hoffman Hershey, married to Barbara Brenneman. Their children are, ———.

Frances Matilda, married to Henry Mayer. Their children are, Dora, Mary Bertha.

Simon Andrew.

Amos, married to Rebecca Bones. Their children are, Florence, Mary Edith.

Rebecca Ann, married to Hebron Herr. Their children are, Emma, Gertrude.

Mary Elisabeth, married to Frank Herr. Their children are, Mabel, Anna.

Emma Susan, married to David L. Gerber. Their children are. Benjamin Franklin.

Martha Jane, married to Cyrus G. Fry.

Barbara Alice; Abraham; Jacob Hoffman.

Susan Hershey, married to Christian Seitz. Their children are, Frances, married to Henry Hoerner. Their children are, Arthur, Edith, Grace, Elmira died young.

(5) Isaac and Rebecca (Hershey) Brubacher begat children, viz:

(6) Mary Ann Brubacher, born July 13th, 1842. She married, in November, 1860, Jonas Mumma, son of John and Fannie (Herr) Mumma. His brothers and sisters are,

Christian Mumma, married to Anna Hoffman. Their children are, Simon, Fianna.

Lizzie Mumma, married to Samuel Erb. Their children are, John, Henry, Lizzie, Mary, Annie.

Fannie Mumma, married to Joseph Hersh. Their children are, John, Henry, Jacob, Christian, Jonas, Fannie.

(6) Jonas and Mary (Brubacher) Mumma begat children, viz:

(7) Eli B. Mumma, born September, 1861.
(7) John B. Mumma, born April, 1863.
(7) Fannie B. Mumma, born September, 1865.
(7) Anna B. Mumma, born June, 1867.
(7) Isaac B. Mumma, born May, 1869.
(7) Ella B. Mumma, born May, 1871.
(6) Andrew H. Brubacher, born June 24th, 1844. He died January 19th, 1867, aged 22 years, 6 months and 25 days.
(6) Susan H. Brubacher, born January 5th, 1847. She died May 28th, 1849, aged 2 years, 4 months and 23 days.
(6) Rebecca H. Brubacher was born November 4th, 1848. She married, in November, 1869, Henry B. Nissly, (born March 28th, 1846), son of Christian E. and Fannie Nissly. His brothers and sisters are mentioned in the "Nissly" family.
(6) Henry B. and Rebecca H. (Brubacher) Nissly begat children, viz:
(7) Alice B. Nissly, born Aug. 5th, 1871.
(7) Isaac B. Nissly, born Oct. 25th, 1872.
(7) Frances B. Nissly, born Aug. 22d, 1874.
(7) Enos B. Nissly, born March 6th, 1876.
(7) Minnie B. Nissly, born June 1st, 1878.
(7) Paris B. Nissly, born June 15th, 1880.
(7) Walter B. Nissly, born Oct. 13th, 1882.
(5) Isaac Brubacher, married the second

time, June 12th, 1856, Anna Herr (widow), daughter of Christian and Esther Herr. Anna Herr was born April 28th, 1818, died April 28th, 1876, aged 57 years, 11 months and 25 days. Her children by her first husband are, Reuben Herr, married to Mary Reidlinger; Amos Herr, married to —— Doerstler; Tobias Herr, married to Elmira Fry; Isaac Herr, married to Anna Coble; John Herr, married to Elisabeth Balmer. Her brothers and sisters are,

Christian Herr, married to Mary Hostetter. Their children are, Fannie, Christian, Susan, Anna, Mary.

John Herr, married to Mary Snyder. Their children are, Mary, Hettie, Fannie.

Susan Herr, married to David Shelly. Their children are, Amos, Eli.

Elisabeth Herr, married to John Sheirich.

Hettie Herr, married to Daniel Bergy.

Mary Herr, married to Abraham Snyder.

Jacob Herr, married to Catharine Lenhart. Their children are, Jacob, Katie.

Catharine Herr, married to Daniel Bergy. Her step brothers and sisters are,

Benjamin Herr, married to Magdalena Newcomer; Fannie Herr, married to John Mumma. Their children are, Christian, Jonas, Lizzie; Fannie Herr, married the second time to Jacob Kreider.

(5) Isaac and Anna (Herr) Brubacher begat children, viz :

(6) Anna H. Brubacher, born March 8th, 1857, died June 10th, 1857, aged 3 months and 2 days.

(6) Isaac H. Brubacher, born June 7th, 1858. He married, in 1878, Lizzie Brubacher, daughter of Christian and Anna (Herr) Brubacher, of Lancaster township, Lancaster Co. Her brothers and sisters are,

Susan, married to Elias Groff. Their children are, Christian, Anna, Lizzie.

Barbara, married to Henry Herr : Fannie ; John ; Mary ; Christian ; Amos ; Henry.

(6) Isaac H. and Lizzie (Brubacher) Brubacher begat children, viz :

(7) Emma B. Brubacher, born October 20th, 1879.

(7) Anna B. Brubacher, born October 3d, 1882.

(6) Esther H. Brubacher, born September 27th, 1860. She married, in 1877, Albert H. Erb, son of Daniel and Catharine (Hernly) Erb. His brothers and sisters are,

Abraham, married to Anna Herr. Their children are, Elmer, Daniel.

Mary ; Henry ; Amos.

(6) Albert H. and Esther H. (Brubacher) Erb, begat children, viz :

(7) Daniel B. Erb, born September 28th, 1878.
(7) Amanda B. Erb, born March 2d, 1880.
(7) Clayton B. Erb, born August 17th, 1881.
(7) Isaac B. Erb, born March 1st, 1883.

(6) Susan Emma H. Brubacher was born January 2d, 1862, died January 19th, 1873, aged 11 years and 17 days.

RETURN AGAIN TO (5) Jacob E. BRUBACHER.

(5) Jacob E. Brubacher was born June 14th, 1821. He married, November 14th, 1849, Elisabeth Hershey, daughter of Andrew and Elisabeth Hershey. She was born June 4th, 1825. Her brothers and sisters are,

Anna Hershey, married to Jacob Snavely. Their children are, Lizzie, Mary, Henry, Andrew, Anna, Jacob, Samuel, Emma, Isaac.

Polly Hershey, married to Jacob Gotschal. Their children are, John, Andrew, Henry, Adam, Eliza.

Jacob Hershey, married to Anna Stehman. Their children are, Emma, Addison, Salinda, Hiram, Anna, Katie, Jacob.

John Hershey, married to Liza Hainly. Their children are, Andrew, Tobias, Anna, Emma. John, Susan, Lizzie.

Henry Hershey, married to Liza Swarr. They had one son, Adam.

Andrew Hershey, married to Susan Kauffman. Their children are, Amos, Martha, Andrew.

Christian Hershey, married to Susan Swarr. Their children are, Ellen, Phares, Susan, Lizzie, John, Fannie, Amanda, Anna, Harvey.

(5) Jacob E. and Elisabeth (Hershey) Brubacher begat children, viz:

(6) Maria H. Brubacher, born May 8th, 1850. She died November 22d, 1880, aged 30 years, 6 months and 14 days. She married, November 7th, 1872, John H. Wissler, born April 6th, 1850, son of Levi and Fanny (Hess) Wissler. His brothers and sisters are, Anna, married to Samuel P. Zimmerman; Barbara, married to Joseph R. Bucher; Levi, married to Martha M. Kreider; Jacob, married to Ella Royer; Katie, married to Dr. Jacob H. Sicling.

(6) John H. and Maria H. (Brubacher) Wissler begat one son, viz:

(7) Jacob B. Wissler was born September 10th, 1873

(6) Benjamin H. Brubacher was born Oc-

tober 26th, 1851. He married, November 13th, 1873, Anna Landis, daughter of Henry and Catharine (Reist) Landis. Her brothers and sisters are, Andrew R. Landis; Benjamin R. Landis, married to Lizzie Rupp; Harry R. Landis, married to Maria Bomberger; Peter R. Landis, married to Priscilla Brubacher; Lizzie R. Landis, married to Harry Miller; Isaac R. Landis, married to Mary L. Brubacher; Jacob R. Landis; Katie R. Landis, married to Jonas Shenk; Ella R. Landis; Clara R. Landis; Israel R. Landis.

(6) Benjamin H. and Anna (Landis) Brubacher begat children, viz:

(7) Emma A. Brubacher, born July 16th, 1875.

(7) Katie Senora Brubacher, born February 15th, 1877.

(7) Andrew Landis Brubacher, born August 15th, 1883.

(6) Andrew H. Brubacher, born March 8th, 1853, died January 30th, 1860, aged 6 years, 10 months and 22 days.

(6) Jacob H. Brubacher, born December 13th, 1854, died July 29th, 1855, aged 7 months and 16 days.

(6) Menno H. Brubacher, born February 26th, 1857. He was married, November 20th, 1877, Catharine Burkholder, daughter

of Jacob and Mary (Bender) Burkholder. Her brothers and sisters are,

Weidler Burkholder.

Annie Burkholder, married to Abraham Lefever. Their children are, Ida, Anna Mary, Aaron.

Jacob Burkholder; Emma Burkholder.

(6) Menno H. and Catharine (Burkholder) Brubacher begat children, viz:

(7) Charlotte B. Brubacher, born January 7th, 1879.

(7) Katie May Brubacher, born May 12th, 1882.

(6) Lizzie H. Brubacher was born November 19th, 1859. She married, November 16th, 1880, Samuel N. Mumma, son of Jonas and Anna (Nissly) Mumma. His brothers and sisters are, Fannie N. Mumma; Jonas N. Mumma, married to Elida Engle; Israel N. Mumma; Amos N. Mumma; John N. Mumma; Anna N. Mumma.

(6) Samuel N. and Lizzie H. (Brubacher) Mumma begat children, viz:

(7) Laura B. Mumma, born November 6th, 1881.

(7) Anna Martha Mumma, born February 22d, 1883.

(6) Ezra H. Brubacher, born July 1st, 1861.

Now return again to (5) Anna E. Brubacher.

(5) Anna E. Brubacher was born June 19th, 1824. She died January 5th, 1873, aged 48 years, 6 months and 16 days. She married, October 5th, 1848, Preacher Abraham Horst, son of Peter and —— Horst, of Lebanon Co., Pa. His brothers and sisters are,

Joseph Horst, married to Veronica Shenk. Their children are, Fannie, Sarah, Peter, Henry, Barbara, Anna, Joseph, Samuel, Catharine.

Catharine Horst, married to Preacher Samuel Gayman, of Juniata Co., Pa. Their children are, Joseph, Molly, Susan, Samuel, Jacob.

Samuel Horst, married to Catharine Stauffer. Their children are, Elisabeth, Sarah, Joseph, Henry, Catharine, John, Samuel, Elias, Anna.

Peter Horst, married to Nancy Shaeffer. Their children are, John, Abraham, Jacob, Anna, Peter.

Jacob Horst, married to Anna B. Krabill.

Elisabeth Horst, married to Peter Smith. Their children are, Adam, Simon, Cyrus, Elizabeth, Monroe, Benjamin, Maria, Joseph.

David Horst, married to Lizzie Breidenstein. Their children are, Simon, Joseph, Anna, Monroe, David.

Sarah Horst, married to Michael Shenk. Their children are, Mary Ann, John, Sarah, Lizzie, Abraham, Elias.

Benjamin Horst, married to Sarah Shaub. Their children are, Mary, Sarah, Anna, Amanda, Malinda, John.

(5) Preacher Abraham and Anna E. (Brubacher) Horst begat children, viz:

(6) Susan B. Horst, born February 5th, 1850. She married Henry M. Shenk, son of John and Martha (Musser) Shenk. His brothers and sisters are, Benjamin M. Shenk, Susan M. Shenk.

(6) Henry M. and Susan B. (Horst) Shenk begat children, viz:

(7) Anna H. Shenk, born October 23d, 1870, died July 14th, 1878, aged 7 years, 8 months and 21 days.

(7) Lizzie H. Shenk, born Oct. 20th, 1871.

(7) John H. Shenk, born Nov. 3d, 1872.

(7) Abraham H. Shenk, born Nov. 7th, 1873.

(7) Susan H. Shenk, born September 23d, 1875, died July 21st, 1878, aged 2 years, 9 months and 28 days.

(7) Magdalena H. Shenk, born October

18th, 1877, died July 20th, 1878, aged 9 months and 2 days.

(7) Mary H. Shenk, born May 5th, 1879.

(7) Henry H. Shenk, born September 3d, 1880.

(7) Benjamin H. Shenk, born November 24th, 1881.

(7) Amos H. Shenk, born February 28th, 1883.

(6) Maria B. Horst, born October 14th, 1851. She married Martin N. Risser, son of Deacon Jacob and Catharine (Nissly) Risser, of Mount Joy township, Lancaster Co., Pa. His brother is, Aaron N. Risser, died.

(6) Martin N. and Maria B. (Horst) Risser begat children, viz:

(7) Catharine H. Risser, born December 31st, 1871.

(7) Tillman H. Risser, born April 9th, 1873, died February 27th, 1874, aged 10 months and 18 days.

(7) Ella H. Risser, born January 12th, 1875.

(7) Lizzie H. Risser, born March 21st, 1876.

(7) Martin H. Risser, born June 16th, 1877.

(7) Abraham H. Risser, born May 21st, 1880.

(7) Jacob H. Risser, born January 11th, 1882.

(7) Menno H. Risser, born May 21st, 1883.

(6) Elizabeth B. Horst, born July 21st, 1853. She was married to Abraham H. Kauffman, son of Christian and Mary Kauffman. His brothers and sisters are, John H. Kauffman, married to —— Shreiner; Fannie H. Kauffman, married David Groff; Mary H. Kauffman; Anna H. Kauffman; —— ——; —— ——.

(6) Abraham H. and Elisabeth B. (Horst) Kauffman begat children, viz:

(7) Harvey H. Kauffman, (7) Ada A. Kauffman, twins, born March 5th, 1875.

(6) Anna B. Horst was born February 14th, 1855. She married Anthony Fauser.

(6) Anthony and Anna B. (Horst) Fauser begat children, viz:

(7) Anna H. Fauser, born Dec. 18th, 1875.

(7) Lizzie H. Fauser, born August 27th, 1877, died October 19th, 1877, aged 1 month and 22 days.

(7) Emma H. Fauser, born July 24th, 1879.

(7) Harry H. Fauser, born May 29th, 1882.

(6) Sarah B. Horst was born November

9th, 1857, died July 18th, 1858, aged 8 months and 9 days.

(6) Catharine B. Horst was born April 22d, 1859. She married Jacob O. Risser, son of Deacon Jacob and Lizzie (Oberholtzer) Risser, of Mount Joy township, Lancaster Co., Pa. His brothers and sisters are, Anna O. Risser, married to Samuel Miller ;Lizzie O. Risser, single.

(6) Jacob O. and Catharine B. (Horst) Risser begat children, viz:

(7) Amos H. Risser, born October 31st, 1880.

(7) John H. Risser, born November 14th, 1883.

(6) Fannie B. Horst was born July 1st, 1861.

(6) Abraham B. Horst was born October 31st, 1862.

(6) Benjamin B. Horst was born August 30th, 1864.

(6) Barbara B. Horst was born February 20th, 1866, died ——.

(6) Martha B. Horst was born March 12th, 1869.

(5) Preacher Abraham Horst was married the second time, June 17th, 1879, to Rebecca Lauber, daughter of Frederick and Mary Lauber, of Perry Co., Pa. Her brothers and sisters are,

Fannie Lauber, married to Jacob H. Lehman. Their children are, Mary, Anna, Isaac, John, Frederick, Daniel.

Baltzar Lauber, married to Mary Kraybill. Their children are, Frederick, Jacob, William, Lizzie, Thomas, Mary Agnes, Simon, Rebecca, John, Lydia.

Mary Lauber, married to Christian Martin. Their children are, Maria, Catharine, Daniel, Lydia, Anna, Emma, Rebecca, Frederick.

Anna Lauber, married to John G. Kraybill. Their children are, Mary, Lydia, Frederick, Simeon, Catharine, John, Benjamin.

Lydia Lauber married to Isaac Winey. Their children are, Frederick, Jacob, Anna, Mary, Fannie.

Susan Lauber, died single.

Catharine Lauber, married to Benjamin Dillman. Their children are, Rebecca, Ida, John, Mary.

Lizzie Lauber, married to Eli Grubb. Their children are, Mary, Frederick, Anna, Jacob, Willie, Rebecca, George.

Simeon Lauber, married to Margarette Grubb. Their children are, Mary, Frederick, Rebecca. Children by second marriage, John, Anna.

Isaac Lauber, died single.

(5) Preacher Abraham and Rebecca (Lauber) Horst begat children, viz :
(6) Naomi L. Horst, born March 4th, 1882.
(5) Elisabeth E. Brubacher was born December 1st, 1826. She died October 27th, 1853, aged 26 years, 10 months and 26 days.

End of (4) Jacob and Maria (Eby) Brubacher's family and connections.

The following is a description of (4)

Jacob Brubacher's brothers and

sisters viz :

(4) John Brubacher was born September 26th, 1783. He died in his ninth year of small-pox.

(4) Henry Brubacher was born October 21st, 1785. He was a merchant for many years. He was familiarly known as "Uncle Henry." He died April 26th, 1839, aged 53 years, 6 months and 5 days.

(4) Christian Brubacher was born September 18th, 1787. He died February 14th, 1853, aged 65 years, 4 months and 24 days. He married, in 1809, Elisabeth Shenk, daughter of John and Elisabeth (Dulabon) Shenk.

Elisabeth Shenk was born in 1789. She

died April 5th, 1873, in her 84th year. Her brothers and sisters are, John Shenk, married to Elisabeth Weidman; Abraham Shenk, died young; Sarah Shenk, married to Jacob Zehrfass; Susan Shenk, died young; Mary Shenk, married to George Gross.

(4) Christian and Elisabeth (Shenk) Brubacher begat children, viz :

(5) Susan S. Brubacher, born in 1810.

(5) Jacob S. Brubacher, born in 1812. He married in 1848, Priscilla Dillman, daughter of Samuel Dillman, Her brother's name is Samuel W. Dillman. He lived in Wilmington, Delaware.

(5) Jacob S. and Priscilla (Dillman) Brubacher begat children, viz:

(6) Elisabeth D. Brubacher, married to David Shreiner. Their children are, (7) Ada.

(6) Mary D. Brubacher, married to Samuel Hess. Their children are, (7) Clara, (7) Ida, (7) Monroe, (7) Emma, (7) Dillman.

(6) Monroe D. Brubacher, married to Alice Zahm. Their children are, (7) Susan.

(6) Albert D. Brubacher, married to Susan Pautz. Their children are, (7) Dillman.

(6) Simon D. Brubacher; (6) Fannie D. Brubacher; (6) Henry D. Brubacher; (6)

Christian D. Brubacher; (6) Susan D. Brubacher.

(5) Elias S. Brubacher was born in 1814. He settled in Canada. There he married Sarah Ores.

(5) Elias S. and Sarah (Ores) Brubacher begat children, viz:

(6) John Brubacher, married to —— Cook.

(6) Christian Brubacher, married to Jeannette Brinkle.

(6) Susan Brubacher, married to Elias Shantz.

(6) Franklin Brubacher, married to Hannah Musselman.

(6) Henry Brubacher; (6) David Brubacher; (6) Lizzie Brubacher; (6) Elias Brubacher; (6) Sarah Ann Brubacher.

(5) John S. Brubacher was born in 1816, died in 1820.

(5) Jonas S. Brubacher was born in 1819. He married Sarah Royer, daughter of Samuel and Sallie (Keller) Royer. Her brothers and sisters are, Jacob Royer, married to Eliza Ream; Philip Royer, married to —— Ream and Catharine Deppi; Samuel Royer, married to Rebecca Stuck; Daniel Royer, married to Polly Lutz; Edward Royer, married to Leah Royer; Polly Royer, mar-

ried to Christian Wenger; Catharine Royer, married to John Keller.

(5) Jonas S. and Sarah (Royer) Brubacher begat children, viz:

(6) Sarah R. Brubacher; (6) Martin R. Brubacher, married to Maria Minnich.

(5) Peter S. Brubacher was born in 1821. He married Eliza Siefritz, of England. They live in Ohio.

(5) Peter S. and Eliza (Siefritz) Brubacher begat children, viz:

(6) Quincy S. Brubacher; (6) Susan S. Brubacher; (6) Lizzie S. Brubacher; (6) Mary S. Brubacher.

(5) Abraham S. Brubacher was born in 1823, died July 5th, 1852.

(5) Christian S. Brubacher was born in 1826. He married Elisabeth Sherk, daughter of John and Lizzie (Kimmel) Sherk.

(5) Christian S. and Elisabeth (Sherk) Brubacher begat children, viz:

(6) Mary Ann Brubacher; (6) Abraham Brubacher, married to Lizzie Roland; (6) John Brubacher; (6) Lizzie Brubacher; (6) Susan Brubacher; (6) Laura Brubacher; (6) Allan Brubacher.

(5) Henry S. Brubacher was born in 1828. He married Eliza Becker, daughter of Henry and Susan (Bucher) Becker. Her brothers and sisters are, John Becker, mar-

ried to Anna Huber.; Elias Becker, married to Anna Stauffer; Henry Becker, married to Anna Bomberger ; Levi Becker, married to Anna Bruckart; Israel Becker, married to Caroline Buckwalter ; Anna Becker, married to Jacob Hess; Catharine Becker, married to John Keener ; Sarah Becker, married to Abraham Hess. Eliza Becker's step brothers and sisters are, Maria, married to Jacob Eby; Fianna, married to Daniel Habecker; Susan, married to Henry Buch; Leah, married to Abraham Bollinger; Amanda, married to Samuel Pautz ; Reuben, married to Amanda Sharp.

(5) Henry S. and Eliza (Becker) Brubacher begat children, viz:

(6) Susan Brubacher, married to Samuel Cockley. Their children are, (7) Noah, (7) Laura, (7) Samuel, (7) Emma, (7) Lizzie.

(6) Christian Brubacher, married to Mary Bomberger. Their children are, (7) Amelia.

(6) Amos Brubacher, married to Magdalena Bomberger. Their children are, (7) Lizzie.

(6) Levi Brubacher; (6) Phares Brubacher ; (6) Ellen Brubacher.

(5) Elisabeth S. Brubacher was born in 1830.

Return again to (4) Maria Brubacher.

(4) Maria Brubacher was born August 6th, 1789. She married Bishop Benjamin Eby. This family is described in the " Eby" family.

(4) Susan Brubacher was born June 20th, 1791. She died November 7th, 1878, aged 87 years, 4 months and 16 days. She married, in September, 1813, John Graybill, son of Michael and Anna (Brubacher) Graybill, of Lebanon Co., Pa.

Michael Graybill was born April 25th, 1748. He died November 1st, 1823, aged 75 years, 6 months and 6 days.

Anna (Brubacher) Graybill was born October 29th, 1756, died October 15th, 1839, aged 82 years, 11 months and 16 days.

John Graybill was born December 18th, 1789, died December 7th, 1838, aged 48 years, 11 months and 19 days. His sisters are,

Fannie Graybill, married to Jacob Weis. They lived in Lebanon Co., Pa. They had nine children, four of whom are still living —one son and three daughters.

Nancy Graybill, married to Henry Pfautz. They lived near Mount Joy, Lancaster Co., Pa. Afterwards in Franklin Co., Pa. They had eight children.

Lizzie Graybill, married to Anthony Capp. They lived at Sheafferstown, Lebanon Co., Pa. Afterwards near Mount Joy, Lancaster Co., Pa. Anthony Capp died there. His widow married Jacob Missimer.

Susan Graybill, married to John Strohm. They lived in Lebanon Co. Afterwards moved to Center Co., Pa. They had a family of six or eight children.

Barbara Graybill, married to John Kreider. They lived in Lebanon Co., then moved to Franklin Co., Pa., and afterwards returned again to Lebanon Co. They had a family of six or eight children.

Catharine Graybill, married to Henry Long. They lived in Lebanon Co., Pa., moved thence to Dayton, Ohio. They had a family of six children.

Mary Graybill, married to John Eby. They lived in Lebanon Co., moved to Center Co., Pa. Had a large family.

(4) John and Susan (Brubacher) Graybill begat children, viz :

(5) Michael B. Graybill was born September 27th, 1814.

(5) Anna B. Graybill was born September 23d, 1816. She married, in 1840, Jacob Horst, son of Peter and Elisabeth Horst. His brothers and sisters are mentioned in the " Brubacher" family.

(5) John B. Graybill was born December 11th, 1817. He married, January 4th, 1838, Catharine Lane, daughter of Joseph and Elisabeth Lane.

Joseph Lane was born February 6th, 1798. His wife, Elisabeth was a daughter of Daniel and Maria Erb. She was born July 25th, 1792, died August 19th, 1865, aged 73 years and 25 days.

Daniel Erb was born April 4th, 1760, died September 29th, 1837, aged 77 years, 5 months and 25 days.

Maria Erb was born July 2d, 1766, died May 10th, 1852, aged 85 years, 10 months and 8 days. The brothers and sisters of Catharine Lane, wife of John B. Graybill are,

Jonas Lane, married to Lucetta Furlow. Had one child named Joseph.

Henry Lane, died single in his 40th year.

Joseph Lane, jr., died single in his 22d year.

(5) John B. and Catharine (Lane) Graybill begat children, viz :

(6) Joseph L. Graybill was born December 24th, 1838. He married, in 1865, Lizzie H. Erisman, daughter of Christian and Catharine Hostetter, of Rapho township, Lancaster Co., Pa. Her brothers and sisters are, Susan Erisman; Metz J. Erisman,

married to Arabella Stauffer; Sarah Erisman; Mary Erisman, married to Benjamin Miller; Albert Erisman, married to Lavina Stehman; Minnie Erisman, married to Elias H. Bomberger; Ellenora Erisman.

(6) Joseph L. and Lizzie H. (Erisman) Graybill begat children, viz:

(7) Mary Catharine Graybill, born August 26th, 1880.

(6) Susan L. Graybill, born September 5th, 1840. She married, February 10th, 1858, Samuel Zug, born February 15th, 1836, son of Abraham and Nancy (Royer) Zug, of Lebanon Co., Pa. His brothers and sisters are, Joseph, married to Mary Wolfelsberger; Lizzie, married to —— Fisher; Lydia, married to Samuel Loos; Rebecca, married to Jacob Nissly; Amanda, married to Hiram Holstein; Abraham, died single.

(6) Samuel and Susan L. (Graybill) Zug begat children, viz:

(7) Lizzie G. Zug, born September 26th, 1859.

(7) Agnes G. Zug, born February 5th, 1861.

(7) Susan G. Zug, born June 29th, 1864.

(7) Graybill G. Zug, born January 3d, 1869.

(7) John G. Zug, (7) Joseph G. Zug,

twins, were born April 21st, 1872. Joseph died June 24th, 1872, aged 2 months and 3 days.

(7) Lane G. Zug, born October 29th, 1874.

(7) Ella Katie G. Zug, born April 10th, 1882.

(6) Mary L. Graybill was born December 16th, 1842, died November 30th, 1858, aged 15 years, 11 months and 14 days.

(6) Anna L. Graybill was born June 24th, 1844. She married, June 6th, 1867, Isaac K. Mumma, (born November 17th, 1844,) son of Isaac and Catharine (Kreider) Mumma. His brothers and sisters are, Mary, married to Levi Brandt; Fannie, married to Henry Hagy; Catharine, married to Samuel Miller; Jacob; Joseph; Caroline, married to Samuel S. Royer.

(6) Isaac K. and Anna L. (Graybill) Mumma begat children, viz:

(7) Graybill G. Mumma, born May 2d, 1869.

(7) Harry H. Mumma, born February 12th, 1881.

(6) Elisabeth L. Graybill was born February 28th, 1847. She married David Kreider, son of David and Sarah (Henry) Kreider. His brothers and sisters are,

Andrew, married to Emma Miller. Their

children are, Sallie, Raymond, Edwin, Annie.

Henry, married to Mary Hoverter. Their children are, Morris D., William H., Mary E.

Joseph, married to Anna Boller. Their children are, Gideon R., Emma S., David A.. Josephine.

Mary Ann, married to Abraham Brightbill. Their children are, Rolandis, Samuel, David, Harry, Sallie, Alice, Ella, Lizzie, Mary, Mabel J.

(6) David and Elisabeth L. (Graybill) Kreider begat children, viz:

(7) John G. Kreider, born March 25th, 1870.

(7) David G. Kreider, born November 13th, 1871.

(7) Joseph Lane Kreider, born July 14th, 1879.

(7) Lizzie G. Kreider, born November 9th, 1880.

(6) Catharine L. Graybill was born August 5th, 1848. She married, November 24th, 1881, Harry S. Risser, son of Peter and Fannie (Stauffer) Risser, of Clay township, Lancaster Co., Pa. His brothers and sisters are, Benjamin, married to Annie Hershey; Mary; Annie, married to Reuben Keller. Their children are, Alvin, Francis, Harvey, Harry.

(6) Sarah L. Graybill was born September 7th, 1851. Died April 27th, 1852, aged 7 months and 20 days.

(6) John L. Graybill was born November 21st, 1853. He married Ida Ream, daughter of Michael Ream. Her brothers and sisters are, Harvey, Susan, Emma, Cora.

(6) John L. and Ida (Ream) Graybill begat children, viz:

(7) Susie R. Graybill, born December 8th, 1880.

RETURN TO (5) JACOB B. GRAYBILL.

(5) Jacob B. Graybill was born August 29th, 1819. He married, October 8th, 1840, Anna Bachman (born June 6th, 1815), daughter of John and Anna (Kreider) Bachman, of Lebanon Co., Pa. Her brothers and sisters are,

Mary Bachman, married to Joseph Longenecker. Their children are, John, Henry, Eliza, Lavina, Mary Ann, Nancy, Leah, Cyrus, Sallie, Joseph, Lydia, Fannie, Emma, Samuel.

Lydia Bachman, married to David Bauman. Their children are, Cyrus, John, Mary Ann, Clara, David, Lizzie.

Christian Bachman, married to Sarah Zinn. Their children are, Malinda, Anna

Maria, George, Catharine, John Z., Fannie, Sarah, Christian Henry, Rosanna, Emma Catharine, Mary A.

Eliza Bachman, died single.

Rosanna Bachman, died single.

Fannie Bachman, married to Henry Bomberger. Their children are, Nancy, Mary, Leah, John H., Simon W., Joseph, Fannie, Henry.

Jacob Bachman, married to Mary Horst. Their children are, Sarah, Anna, Simon W., Jacob H., John Q., Aaron P., David H., Pennrose F., Mary Jane, A. Lincoln, Rosanna. Jacob Bachman married the second time, Christiana Miller.

Cyrus Bachman, married to Catharine Hoffer. Their children are, Mary Ellen, Villarah, Alice, Nancy, Reuben H., Elisabeth, Lydia A., George H., Cyrus A., Annie Grace, John.

Sallie Bachman, married to John Forney. Their children are, Clara, Sarah, Jacob. She married, the second time, Henry Gingrich. Their children are, Nancy, Lizzie, John H., Mary, Sallie.

Leah Bachman, married to John Carper. Their children are, Rosanna, Emeline, Mary A.

John Bachman, married to Elisabeth

Snavely. Their children are, William A., Mary, Joseph S., Lizzie S., John H., Sallie.

Michael Bachman, married to Sarah Landis. Their children are, Levi H., Emma, Rolandis, Sarah, Frank, Katie, Ida, Fannie, Michael, Susan.

(5) Jacob B. and Anna (Bachman) Graybill begat children, viz :

(6) Mary Ann Graybill, born August 3d, 1841. She married, August 11th, 1859, Samuel K. Slabach (born March 11th, 1841), son of Samuel H. and Susanna (Keller) Slabach. His brothers and sisters are, Adam K. Slabach.

(6) Samuel K. and Mary Ann (Graybill) Slabach begat children, viz:

(7) Edwin G. Slabach, born March 7th, 1861.

(7) Franklin G. Slabach, born October 3d, 1863.

(7) Villarah G. Slabach, born June 15th, 1865.

(7) Susan G. Slabach, born December 18th, 1866.

(6) John Graybill was born December 8th, 1842, died March 12th, 1843, aged 3 months and 4 days.

(6) Sarah Graybill was born August 2d, 1844, died March 31st, 1850, aged 5 years, 7 months and 29 days.

(6) Henry Graybill was born June 4th, 1846, died September 16th, 1877, aged 31 years, 3 months and 12 days. He married, December 24th, 1872, Barbara Snavely, (born March 19th, 1844), daughter of Jacob and Barbara (Nissly) Snavely. Her brothers and sisters are, John, Annie, Jacob, Solomon, Martin, Susan.

(6) Henry and Barbara (Snavely) Graybill begat children, viz:

(7) One, still born; (7) Jacob Franklin Graybill, born June 10th, 1874; (7) Cora Agnes Graybill, born July 10th, 1876, died August 10th, 1880, aged 4 years and 1 month; (7) Harry S. Graybill, born April 6th, 1878.

(6) Susan Graybill was born October 20th, 1848. She married, August 28th, 1867, Daniel G. Struphar, (born June 12th, 1848), son of Isaac and Elisabeth (Frank) Struphar. His brothers and sisters are, Mary C. Struphar, married to John L. Wenger.

(6) Daniel G. and Susan (Graybill) Struphar begat children, viz:

(7) Mary J. Struphar, born Nov. 2d, 1869.
(7) Isaac G. Struphar, born Nov. 3d, 1871.
(7) Jacob G. Struphar, born January 10th, 1875.

(7) John Henry Struphar, born March 26th, 1877.

(7) Daniel Nathan Struphar, born March 21st, 1879.

(6) Nancy Graybill was born October 15th, 1850. She married, October 4th, 1870, Daniel W. Wenger (born February 22d, 1850), son of —— ——. His brothers and sisters are, David, Lydia, Leah, Lizzie.

(6) Daniel W. and Nancy (Graybill) Wenger begat children, viz:

(7) David G. Wenger, born April 8th, 1871.

(7) Henry G. Wenger, born July 13th, 1872.

(7) Harvey G. Wenger, born December 6th, 1873.

(7) Jacob G. Wenger, born September 5th, 1875.

(7) Ida G. Wenger, born November 10th, 1877.

(7) Daniel G. Wenger, born March 1st, 1881.

(6) Jacob Graybill was born December 11th, 1853, died April 19th, 1871, aged 17 years, 4 months and 8 days.

(6) Michael Graybill was born February 28th, 1855. He married, October 7th, 1876, Mary Light (born March 12th, 1857), daughter of Jeremiah and Elisabeth (Krei-

der) Light. Her brothers are, Joseph K. and Daniel K.

(6) Michael and Mary (Light) Graybill begat children, viz :

(7) Jeremiah Graybill, born August 20th, 1878, died April 5th, 1879, aged 7 months and 15 days.

(7) Michael Graybill, born November 18th, 1879.

(6) Leah Graybill, born September 1857. She married September 11th, 1875, Joseph K. Light (born August 2d, 1853), son of Jeremiah and Elisabeth (Kreider) Light.

(6) Jospeh K. and Leah (Graybill) Light begat children, viz :

(7) Harry A. Light, born October 31st, 1877.

(7) Irwin G. Light, born November 9th, 1879, died December 14th, 1879, aged 1 month and 5 days.

(7) Ida Light and (7) Graybill Light were born June 16th, 1881, both died young.

(7) Nancy B. Light, born July 20th, 1882.

RETURN AGAIN TO (5) SUSAN B. GRAYBILL.

(5) Susan B. Graybill was born December 1st, 1822, died October 24th, 1823, aged 10 months and 23 days.

(5) Samuel B. Graybill was born October 17th, 1824, lived only 6 days.

(5) Henry B. Graybill was born October 15th, 1825. He married, October 9th, 1848, Elisabeth Deppen (born December 8th, 1826), daughter of Samuel and Mary (Royer Deppen. Her brothers and sisters are,

Catharine Deppen married Philip Royer. Their children are, Henry, Samuel, Fianna, Matilda.

Isaac Deppen married Rebecca Zook. Their children are, Sarah, Frank, Wallace. Isaac Deppen married, second time, Catharine Tobias. Their children are, Wellington, Anna, Emma, Elisabeth, Oscar.

Mary Deppen married Abraham Landis. Their children are, Mary, Emeline, Levi, Sarah.

Matilda Deppen married Christian Hostetter. Their children are, Jemima, Sarah, Emma, Edwin, Frank, Joseph.

John Deppen married Sarah Shelkammer. Their children are, Mary, Samuel, George.

Sarah Deppen married Abraham Gibble. Their children are, Isaac, Leah, Emma, John, Samuel, Lydia, Abraham, Ira, Jacob.

Anna Deppen married Richard Linebach. Their children are, Emma, Morris, Lizzie, Frank, Harvey.

Lydia Deppen married Lewis Peiffer. Their children are, Edwin, Lizzie.

Samuel Deppen, married Mary Seltzer. Their children are, Ella, May, Laura.

(5) Henry B. and Elisabeth (Deppen) Graybill begat children, viz:

(6) Emma Elisabeth Graybill, born October 9th, 1849, died in 1852, aged 3 years.

(6) John Graybill born September 27th, 1851. He married, in October, 1873, Salinda Graybill, daughter of Isaac H. and Fianna (Raupp) Graybill. Her brothers and sisters are, John R. Graybill, married to Elmira Becker; Catharine R. Graybill, married to Jacob Graybill; Phares R. Graybill, married to Emma Graybill; Daniel R. Graybill, married to Sabilla Baer; Clara R. Graybill, married to Harry Seldomridge.

(6) John D. and Salinda (Graybill) Graybill begat children, viz:

(7) Salinda M. Graybill, born February 27th, 1875. The mother died March 8th, 1875.

(6) John D. Graybill, married the second time, January 16th, 1877, Barbara Hertzler, daughter of John and Fannie (Erb) Hertzler, of Cumberland Co., Pa. Her brothers and sisters are, Mary Hertzler, married to Joseph Ruhl; Abraham Hertzler, married to Fannie Strickler; John Hertzler, married

to Jane Hollinger; Annie Hertzler, married to Preacher Jacob M. Herr; Daniel Hertzler, married to Fannie Hastings; Henry Hertzler.

(6) John D. and Barbara (Hertzler) Graybill begat children, viz:

(7) Deppen Graybill, born in January, 1881; died young.

(7) Harry Graybill, born July 26th, 1882.

(6) Samuel D. Graybill was born March 11th, 1853. He married, April 11th, 1878, Effie J. Holl, daughter of Joseph and Barbara (Carpenter) Holl. Her brothers and sisters are, Lillian Holl; Ellen Holl; Florence Holl, married to Joseph Long; Clara Holl, married to Isaac Bachman; Carpenter Holl.

(6) Rufus D. Graybill, born January 11th, 1855.

(5) Isaac Graybill, born April 30th, 1833, died March 8th, 1854, aged 20 years, 10 months and 8 days.

RETURN AGAIN TO (4) JOHN BRUBACHER.

(4) John Brubacher (Deacon), (this one was also named John, the first John having died), was born July 11th, 1793. He died October 10th, 1875, aged 82 years, 2 months and 29 days. He emigrated to

Canada in 1816. There he married, March 6th, 1817, Catharine Sherk, daughter of Joseph and Mary (Betzner) Sherk. Her brothers and sisters are, Joseph Sherk, married to Ann Thornton; Susan Sherk, married to John Thornton; Lydia Sherk, married to Morgan Thomson; Martha Sherk, married to David Codling; Elisabeth Sherk, married to —— Wood; Jacob Sherk, marrried to —— ——; John Sherk, married to —— Thornton; Samuel Sherk, married to Martha Brech; Polly Sherk, died single; Preacher David Sherk, married to Elisabeth Betzner. Catharine Sherk was born February 11th. 1798. She died October 8th, 1882, aged 84 years, 7 months and 27 days.

(4) Deacon John and Catharine (Sherk) Brubacher begat children, viz:

(5) Jacob Brubacher was born April 9th, 1818. He married, in 1840, Mary Weaver, daughter of Benjamin and Veronica (Martin) Weaver. Her brothers and sisters are, Henry Weaver; Anna Weaver, married to Elias Eby; David Weaver, married to Catharine Eby; Benjamin Weaver, married to Anna Shantz; John Weaver, married to Susan Brubacher; Joseph Weaver, married to Veronica Shantz.

(5) Jacob and Mary (Weaver) Brubacher begat children, viz:

(6) Susanna Brubacher, married to George B. Smith. Their children are, (7) Mary, (7) Sarah, (7) Jacob, (7) Lizzie, (7) Susanna.

(5) Susanna Brubacher was born June 28th, 1819. She married, in 1839, John Weaver, son of Benjamin and Veronica (Martin) Weaver, already mentioned above.

(5) John and Susanna (Brubacher) Weaver begat children, viz:

(6) Veronica Weaver, married to Benjamin Horst. Their children are, (7) Susanna, (7) Mary.

(5) Elisabeth Brubacher was born December 13th, 1820. She married, in 1842, Jonas Bingeman, son of John and Hannah (Bergy) Bingeman. His brothers and sisters are, Judith Bingeman, married to John Snyder; Abram Bingeman, died young; Esther Bingeman, married to George Kraft; Susan Bingeman, married to Rudolph Detweiler; John Bingeman, died young; Hannah Bingeman, married to Preacher Elias Snyder; Catharine Bingeman, married to Noah Ziegler; Mary Bingeman, married to Jacob Eby; Magdalena Bingeman, married to Joseph Eby; Isaac Bingeman, died young; John Bingeman, married to Judith

Snyder and Elisabeth Clemens; Sarah Bingeman, married to Peter Wile; Isaac Bingeman, married to Sarah Shoemaker.

(5) Jonas and Elisabeth (Brubacher) Bingeman begat children, viz:

(6) John Bingeman, married to Catharine Snyder. Their children are, (7) Alfred, (7) Edwin, (7) Lydia Ann, (7) Emma, (7) Hannah, (7) Maria.

(6) Menno Bingeman, died young.

(6) Joseph Bingeman, married to Leah Hallman. Their children are, (7) Sylvia Maria, (7) Melissa Elma, (7) Ida Bertha, (7) Alivia, (7) Milton.

(6) Elias Bingeman, married to Amanda Eby. Their children are, (7) Angus, (7) Melinda, (7) David, (7) Lizzie, (7) Melvin.

(6) Hannah Bingeman, married to Menno Weaver. Their children are, (7) Ida, (7) Irwin.

(6) Catharine Bingeman.

(6) Veronica Bingeman, married to Moses B. Shantz. Their children are, (7) Edgar, (7) Lizzie, (7) Allson.

(6) Jonas Bingeman, married to Lillie Oberholtzer.

(6) Lizzie Bingeman.

(5) John Brubacher was born August 9th, 1822. He married Magdalena Musselman and Esther (Musselman) Martin Widow,—

both daughters of David and Esther (Martin) Musselman. Their brothers and sisters are, Anna Musselman, married David Bauman ; Peter Musselman, married to Elisabeth Snyder ; Daniel Musselman, died young ; David Musselman, married to Magdalena Brubacher ; Mary Musselman, married to Henry Brubacher ; John Musselman, married to Susan Snyder and Amanda Lichty; Lydia Musselman, married to Samuel Brubacher ; Solomon Musselman, married to Barbara Martin; Leah Musselman, married to Absalom Martin ; Elisabeth Musselman, married to Moses Brubacher.

(5) John and Magdalena (Musselman) Brubacher begat children, viz:

(6) Mary Ann Brubacher, married to David M. Martin. Their children are, (7) Amanda, (7) Leander, (7) Reuben.

(6) David Brubacher, married to Susan Sittler. Their children are, (7) Addison, (7) Velina, (7) Lavina, (7) Malinda, (7) Allan, (7) Ida, (7) Alexander, (7) Albert, (7) John.

(6) Nancy Brubacher, married to Levi Groff. Their children are, (7) Magdalena.

(6) Magdalena Brubacher, married to Samuel Snyder. Their children are, (7) Malinda, (7) John Alvin, (7) Samuel Edwin.

(6) Tillman Brubacher, married to Louisa

Cressman. Their children are, (7) Magdalena, (7) Erwin.

(6) Susan Brubacher, married to Peter Eby. Their children are, (7) Elsie Laura.

(6) John Brubacher, married to Angeline Rudy. Their children are, (7) Edwin.

(6) Benjamin Brubacher; (6) Martin Brubacher; (6) Enoch Brubacher; (6) Noah Brubacher; (6) Amanda Brubacher; (6) Harriet Brubacher; (6) Leah Brubacher, died young.

(5) Henry Brubacher was born February 12th, 1824. He married, in 1852, Mary Musselman, daughter of David and Esther (Martin) Musselman. Her brothers and sisters have been mentioned above.

(5) Henry and Mary (Musselman) Brubacher begat children, viz:

(6) Magdalena Brubacher, married to Martin Weaver. Their children are, (7) Mary, (7) Simon, (7) Abraham, (7) Louisa.

(6) Hettie Brubacher, married to Moses Weber.

(6) Susanna Brubacher.

(6) Mary Brubacher.

(6) Isaac Brubacher, married to Mary Ann Betzner. Their children are, (7) Salinda, (7) Isaac.

(6) Henry Brubacher; (6) Joseph Bru-

bacher; (6) Solomon Brubacher; (6) Catharine Brubacher; (6) John Brubacher.

(5) Joseph Brubacher was born October 27th, 1825. He died in 1841.

(5) Christian Brubacher was born April 27th, 1827. He died in 1848.

(5) Samuel Brubacher was born January 4th, 1829. He married, in 1862, Lydia Musselman, daughter of David and Esther (Martin) Musselman. Her brothers and sisters have been mentioned.

(5) Samuel and Lydia (Musselman) Brubacher begat children, viz:

(6) Hettie Brubacher, married to Benjamin M. Eby. Their children are, (7) Phares.

(6) Simeon Brubacher; (6) Rebecca Brubacher; (6) Sarah Brubacher; (6) Mary Brubacher; (6) Lydia Brubacher; (6) Ephraim Brubacher; (6) Manassa Brubacher; (6) Samuel Brubacher.

(5) Magdalena Brubacher was born January 14th, 1831. Lived only 2 months and 11 days.

(5) Anna Brubacher was born September 19th, 1832. She married, in 1853, Jacob Y. Shantz, son of Jacob and Polly (Yost) Shantz. His brothers and sisters are, Isaac Y. Shantz, married to Catharine Clemens; John Y. Shantz, married to Susan Shirich;

Veronica Y. Shantz, married to Abram D. Clemens; Joshua Y. Shantz, married to Magdalena Martin; Joseph Y. Shantz, married to Elisabeth Y. Stauffer; David Y. Shantz, married to Barbara Stauffer; Samuel Y. Shantz, married to Esther Erb; Amos Y. Shantz, married to Nancy Moyer.

(5) Jacob Y. and Anna (Brubacher) Shantz begat children, viz:

(6) Susanna Shantz, married to Tillman G. Moyer. Their children are, (7) Milton, (7) Susanna.

(6) Jacob B. Shantz, married to Catharine Hipple.

(6) Tillman Shantz.

(6) John Shantz, married to Joanna Bauman. Their children are, (7) Leander.

(6) Mary Shantz, married to Noah B. Detweiler.

(6) Ida Shantz; (6) Ernice Shantz.

(5) Magdalena Brubacher was born March 10th, 1834. She married, in 1852, David Musselman, son of David and Esther (Martin) Musselman. His brothers and sisters have been mentioned.

(5) David and Magdalena (Brubacher) Musselman begat children, viz:

(6) Hannah Musselman, married to Franklin Brubacher.

(6) Levi Musselman; (6) Catharine Mus-

selman; (6) Daniel Musselman; (6) Lydia Musselman; (6) Mary Musselman; (6) Solomon Musselman; (6) Susanna Musselman; (6) David Musselman; (6) John Musselman; (6) Magdalena Musselman; (6) Elisabeth Musselman; (6) Rebecca Musselman.

(5) Mary Brubacher was born August 29th, 1836. She married, in 1855, Moses Martin, son of John and Anna (Weaver) Martin. His brothers and sisters are, Elisabeth Martin, married to Peter Shantz; Abraham Martin (Bishop). married to Elizabeth Bauman; Anna Martin, married to Amos Cressman; Judith Martin, married to George Bauman; Lydia Martin, married to Menno Cressman; Veronica Martin, married to Isaac Snyder; Magdalena Martin, married to Peter Sherk; Rebecca Martin, married to Menno Gingrich; Mary Martin, married to Enoch Bauman; Enos Martin, married to Anna Weaver and Sarah Bauman; Susanna Martin, married to Enoch Bauman.

(5) Moses and Mary (Brubacher) Martin begat children, viz:

(6) Tillman Martin, married to Mary Shantz. Their children are, (7) Lovina.

(6) John Martin, died young.

(5) Catharine Brubacher was born July

5th, 1838. She married, in 1855, David Betzner, son of John and Magdalena (Eby) Betzner. His brothers and sisters are, Noah Betzner, married to Barbara Snyder; Moses Betzner, married to Veronica Brubacher; Elisabeth Betzner, married to Joseph C. Snyder; Leah Betzner; Mary Betzner, married to Levi C. Snyder.

(5) David and Catharine (Brubacher) Betzner begat children, viz:
(6) John Betzner; (6) Josiah Betzner, married to Millie Moyer. Their children are, (7) Cora May.
(6) Henry Betzner; (6) David Betzner; (6) Eliab Betzner; (6) Benjamin Betzner.

(5) Benjamin Brubacher was born April 24th, 1841. He married, in 1867, Barbara Myer, daughter of John and Mary (Wenger) Myer. Her brothers and sisters are, Dianna Myer, married to Henry Whitmer; Louisa Myer, married to Henry Rudy, William Studs and —— Stauffer; Eliab Myer, married to Sarah Daws; Solomon Myer, married to Caroline Krauter; Isaac Myer, married to Alice Francesco; Sarah Myer, married to Zimmerman Martin and David Snyder; Eliza Myer, married to Isaac L. Bowman; Hannah Myer, married to Aaron Bowman; Mary Ann Myer, married to Horace Freeland; Absalom Myer,

married to Lovina Moyer; John Myer, married to Angeline Snyder; Aaron Myer, died young.

(5) Benjamin and Barbara (Myer) Brubacher begat children, viz:

(6) Albert Brubacher; (6) Josephus Brubacher.

(5) Veronica Brubacher was born May 16th, 1843. She married, in 1863, Moses Betzner, son of John and Magdalena (Eby) Betzner. His brothers and sisters have been mentioned before.

(5) Moses and Veronica (Brubacher) Betzner begat children, viz :

(6) Lucinda Betzner; (6) John Betzner; (6) Magdalena Betzner; (6) Allan Betzner; (6) Elisabeth Betzner.

(6) Moses Brubacher married Elisabeth Musselman. Their children are, (7) Amos, (7) Menno, (7) Susanna (7) Moses, (7) Lucinda, (7) Israel.

(6) Christian Brubacher married Lydia Good. Their children are, (7) Sarah, (7) Jacob.

married to Lovina Moyer; John Myer, married to Angeline Snyder; Aaron Myer, died young.

(5) Benjamin and Barbara (Myer) Brubacher begat children, viz:

(6) Albert Brubacher; (6) Josephus Brubacher.

(5) Veronica Brubacher was born May 16th, 1843. She married, in 1863, Moses Betzner, son of John and Magdalena (Eby) Betzner. His brothers and sisters have been mentioned before.

(5) Moses and Veronica (Brubacher) Betzner begat children, viz:

(6) Lucinda Betzner; (6) John Betzner; (6) Magdalena Betzner; (6) Allan Betzner; (6) Elisabeth Betzner.

INDEX.

(1) Brubacher John.. 5
(2) Brubacher Daniel and his descendants..... 7
(2) Brubacher John—birth, marriage and death.. 11
Birth, marriage and death of children........... 11
(3) Brubacher Jacob and Susan. The family of, as follows..14, 15
(4) Brubacher Jacob and Maria, birth, marriage and death.................................17, 18
Birth, &c., of their children and their respective families.................................... 72
(5) Susan E. Brubacher ....72—76
(5) Mary Brubacher.................................76—86
(5) Catharine Brubacher........................86—88
(5) Sem Brubacher....................................88, 151
(5) Henry E. Brubacher........................186, 188
(5) Isaac Brubacher..............................194—199
(5) Jacob E. Brubacher.........................199—202
(5) Anna E. Brubacher..........................202—207
(5) Elisabeth Brubacher.............................209
(4) Brubacher John......................................209
(4) Brubacher Henry...................................209
(4) Brubacher Christian and Elisabeth, birth, marriage and death. 209, 210
Birth, &c., of their children and their respective families....................................210, 213
(4) Brubacher Maria married to Bishop Benjamin Eby..213
(4) Brubacher Susan married to John Graybill, birth, marriage and death...............214
Birth, &c., of their children and their respective families...................................214—220

Brubacher John and Catharine, birth,
marriage, and death............................. 228
rth, etc., of their children and their respect-
ive families .... 229—239
mberger Christian........................... 113
mberger Joseph and Magdalena 113
Bomberger (Bishop) Christian and Barbara, birth, marriage and death........113, 114
rth, &c., of their children and their respect-
ive families..114—119
Bomberger Elisabeth married to Jacob
Gingrich, birth, marriage and death........ 119
rth, &c., of their children and their respective families................................. 119—121
Bomberger Magdalena married to Preach-
er Christian Nissly........ 121
Bomberger Maria married to Christian
Weaver, birth, marriage and death.........121
mes of their children and their respective
families 122
Bomberger (Preacher) Joseph and Sarah,
birth, marriage and death....... 122
rth, &c., of their children and their respect-
ive families.... .... 123—129
Bomberger John and Catharine, birth,
marriage and death......... 129
rth, &c., of their children and their respective families...................................129—134
Bomberger Barbara married to Jacob
Wissler, birth, marriage and death.........134
rth, &c., of their children and their respect-
ive families..135—137
Bomberger Anna married to Martin Nissly.137
cher Joseph married to Elisabeth Eby.
Descendants of ....19—21
rkholder family..................................53—56

(1) Eby Theodore 18
(2) Eby Christian and Elisabeth.................. 18
Birth and marriage of family......................18, 19
(3) Eby Christian and Catharine 19
Birth, marriage, and death of their children,
    and their childrens' families..............19—23
(4) Elisabeth Eby married to Joseph Bucher
                                                          19—21
(4) Christian Eby married to Veronica Hershey..21—30
(4) Peter Eby (Bishop) married to Margarette Hess..30—39
(4) John Eby, married to Mary Wittwer...39—52
(4) Andrew Eby married to Elisabeth Stauffer
                                                          52, 53
(4) Catharine Eby married to Abraham Burkholder......................................53—56
(4) Barbara Eby married to Joseph Snyder.56—60
(4) Anna Eby married to Jacob Wissler.....61—62
(4) Benjamin Eby (Bishop) married to Maria
    Brubacher ....62—72
(1) Hammaker John and Maria.................... 165
(2) Hammaker Daniel and Anna, birth, marriage and death................................... 165
Birth, marriage and death of their children,
    and their respective families 165
(3) Anna Hammaker married to David K
    Stauffer........................156, 166, 171—178
(3) Daniel Hammaker married to Frances
    Forry ....166—171
(3) Mary Hammaker and Barbara Hammaker.171
Kauffman Michael and Veronica.................. 163
Kauffman Andrew and Adaline.................... 184
(1) Nissly Jacob (came from Germany)......... 88
(2) Nissly John... 88

(3) Nissly (Bishop) Samuel and Barbara, birth, marriage and death............... .. 90
Birth, marriage and death of their children, and their respective families........... 90—113
(4) John Nissly (Preacher) married to Anna Hershey................................90—96
(4) Martin Nissly married to Anna Bomberger 113, 137—142
(4) Samuel Nissly married to Anna Eby...96—105
(4) Christian Nissly (Preacher) married to Magdalena Bomberger.................105—108
(4) Jacob Nissly married to Barbara Wittwer 108—111
(4) Henry Nissly married to Maria Nissly.111, 112
(4) Veronica Nissly married to Abraham Huber and Jonas Eby.....................112
(1) Stauffer Christian............................156
(2) Stauffer John and Barbara, birth, marriage and death..................................157
Birth, marriage and death of their children, and their respective families...............157
(3) John Stauffer married to —— Kolb. 158
(3) Jacob Stauffer married to Anna Nissly......158
(3) Joseph Stauffer married to Catharine Acker 159
(3) Christian Stauffer. (3) Anna Stauffer.162, 163
(3) Barbara Stauffer married to Christian Knull 163
(3) Maria Stauffer married to Henry Acker....163
(3) Christian Stauffer..............................163
(3) Martin Stauffer married to Maria Kauffman 156, 163
Wissler family.............................61, 62

ADDENDA.

Page 41. Elisabeth K. Nissley married David Rutt.

Page 41. Ann K. Nissley married Jacob Good.

Page 167. The children of Harry and Anna (Forry) Heise died in infancy.

ERRATA.

Page 101. The children of Franklin L., and Lillie H. (Hoffman) Nissley are, (7) Harry, (7) Edith May, not Eda.

Page 102, Levi Forrey should be Levi Forney.

Page 107. Samuel Schlott was not a preacher, his father was.

www.ingramcontent.com/pod-product-compliance
Lightning Source LLC
Chambersburg PA
CBHW020806230426
43666CB00007B/888